The Manager as Leader

The Manager as Leader

B. Keith Simerson and Michael L. Venn

The Manager as...

Jerry W. Gilley, Series Editor

Westport, Connecticut
London

Library of Congress Cataloging-in-Publication Data

Simerson, Byron K.
The manager as leader / B. Keith Simerson and Michael L. Venn.
    p. cm. — (The manager as ...)
    Includes bibliographical references and index.
    ISBN 0–275–99010–9
    1. Leadership—Handbooks, manuals, etc. 2. Management—Handbooks,
manuals, etc. I. Venn, Michael L. II. Title. III. Series.
HD57.7.S524 2006
658.4′092—dc22   2006007249

British Library Cataloguing in Publication Data is available.

Library of Congress Catalog Card Number: 2006007249
ISBN: 0–275–99010–9
ISSN: 1555–7480

First published in 2006

Praeger Publishers, 88 Post Road West, Westport, CT 06881
An imprint of Greenwood Publishing Group, Inc.
www.praeger.com

Printed in the United States of America

The paper used in this book complies with the
Permanent Paper Standard issued by the National
Information Standards Organization (Z39.48–1984).

10 9 8 7 6 5 4 3 2 1

Trademark Notice

The term "Contextual Leadership Model" used throughout this book is a trademark of Tradewinds Consulting, LLC (305 Ridgeway, Kohler, WI 53044).

The terms "Manitowoc" and "Crane CARE" used in this book are registered trademarks of The Manitowoc Company, Inc. (2400 S. 44th Street, Manitowoc, WI 54221).

The term "Situational Leadership" used in this book is the registered trademark of The Ken Blanchard Companies (125 State Place, Escondido, CA 92029).

To Darlie, you are a leader in all that you do. To Jarrett, Brent, and Andrew, your boundless enthusiasm, tenacity, and creativity inspire me. To Kristin, our conversations are never dull and your observations are always insightful.
—B.K.S.

To my father, Ray, who taught me how to respect other people, my mother, Pat, who taught me how to care for other people, and my brother, Raymond, who provided a great example to follow. To Diane, my wife, who taught me what is important in life and my children Chris, Nick, and Ray, who taught me how to say "I love you" every morning when I wake up and every night before I go to bed. You have all been leaders in my life.
—M.L.V.

Contents

PART III
Action Plan, Tools, and Resources

Publisher's Note

The backbone of every organization, large or small, is its managers. They guide and direct employees' actions, decisions, resources, and energies. They serve as friends and leaders, motivators and disciplinarians, problem solvers and counselors, partners and directors. Managers serve as liaisons between executives and employees, interpreting the organization's mission and realizing its goals. They are responsible for performance improvement, quality, productivity, strategy, and execution—through the people who work for and with them. All too often, though, managers are thrust into these roles and responsibilities without adequate guidance and support. MBA programs provide book learning but little practical experience in the art of managing projects and people; at the other end of the spectrum, exceptional talent in one's functional area does not necessarily prepare the individual for the daily rigors of supervision. This series is designed to address those gaps directly.

The Manager as ... series provides a unique library of insights and information designed to help managers develop a portfolio of outstanding skills. From Mentor to Marketer, Politician to Problem Solver, Coach to Change Leader, each book provides an introduction to the principles, concepts, and issues that define the role; discusses the evolution of recent and current trends; and guides readers through the dynamic process of assessing their strengths and weaknesses and creating a personal development plan. Featuring diagnostic tools, exercises, checklists, case examples, practical tips, and recommended resources, the books in this series will help readers at any stage in their careers master the art and science of management.

Preface

We work with leaders in a number of organizations, professions, and industries. Over time, we have come to realize that leaders have a lot in common: they typically face a myriad of challenges, function within an assortment of conditions, and grapple with a variety of circumstances. To complicate the matter, these factors continually shift causing the context in which these leaders function to constantly change.

Although we realize there has been much recent press around the unethical and illegal acts perpetrated by a few of the U.S. corporate leaders, each and every one of the leaders we have come to know are sincerely committed to doing their part in helping their organizations and their people succeed. In some cases, in just the number of hours they work each day, it is obvious that they willingly sacrifice themselves to make their and their organization's vision become a reality.

In working with and observing leaders, we have also come to notice they frequently end the day exhausted from dealing with the breadth of assumptions, needs, and expectations held of them as leaders. This book is written to help these friends of ours—the ones we have made, the ones we are yet to make, and the ones we may never meet:

- Address the breadth of expectations followers have of them
- Influence others to perform more effectively and efficiently than they thought possible
- Navigate through constantly changing contexts in a manner that ensures they are focusing their leadership decisions and actions to achieve optimal impact
- Attain the success they, as leaders, desire

Because we understand how busy today's leaders are, this book contains guides, checklists, and worksheets to help the reader easily understand and apply the information we present. We also use six case studies to illustrate contextual leadership in action. These case studies feature a variety of organizations representing public corporations, private corporations, nonprofit and not-for-profit organizations, the federal government, state government, and religious institutions.

These case studies come from leaders willing to take time out of their busy schedules to share their stories with us; without their kindness and generosity this book would not have been possible. For this, we thank Derek Carissimi, Roy Morris, Dr. Martha Stanford, and Larry Weyers. Conversations with—and support and assistance from—others influenced our thinking and also helped make this book possible. For this, we thank Dr. Bruce Lane, Michael Marchi, Dan Trudell, Monica Trudell, Rev. Jim Hollister, Bill Schult Sr., Dr. Mark Mone, and David Fortson.

PART I

Principles and Practices

ONE

Overview

THE "RIGHT" OF LEADERSHIP

In the past, there were two requirements to becoming a leader. First, only a small percentage of individuals were considered to have the "right stuff" to serve as a leader. By natural design or happenstance, they had the mental, emotional, and physical capacity to think and act as leaders. Then, only a small number within this group were considered to have the "right" to serve as a leader. This was earned by being the right gender, having the right family heritage, being from the right socioeconomic position, or attending the right school. The exceptions to this rule were those "self-made men" who were smart enough to invent products or launch new services at the right time and thus be raised to the leadership level. In this context, managers were not considered leaders but rather people who communicated the leader's directives (orders) to the followers (workers).

More recently, a small percentage of individuals "high enough" in the organizational hierarchy were called leaders. Those on one side of this invisible line were followers and those inherently capable of successfully making the leap crossed to the other side of the line where they had the "right" to be considered leaders. In this context, managers—frequently called middle managers—straddled the line of leadership. Those below them looked on them as leaders and frequently blamed them for the unrealistic expectations of upper leadership, while upper leadership expected them (the managers) to enforce their expectations and blamed them if those expectations (regardless of how realistic or unrealistic) were not successfully achieved. These middle managers were crucial to the success of the organization, as they were the "greasers of the organizational wheel," making certain things happened smoothly.

Many factors, including heightened global competition and the gradual lessening of national boundaries in the business world, led to two decades of downsizings and rightsizings. During this time, countless middle managers lost their jobs, and the distinction between leader and nonleader became completely blurred.

For those remaining managers, the nature of their jobs had significantly changed. In the past, many considered them to be responsible only for managerial activities such as planning, organizing, staffing, coordinating, reporting, budgeting, and evaluation. The nature of supervisory positions also changed. In the past, many considered them to be responsible only for supervisory activities; they assigned tasks, monitored employee performance, provided performance feedback, and dispensed rewards/recognition when appropriate and disciplinary action when needed. But the events of the past decades forever changed the role managers and supervisors are expected to play—individuals throughout an organization are now *called on* (some frequently, others sporadically or periodically) to think and act like a leader.

The pace of change in the business environment continues to accelerate. The external contexts within which organizations operate, as well as their internal contexts, constantly shift. Start-up organizations can quickly become the status quo. Status quo organizations must constantly reinvent themselves and act more like start-ups. Change is the norm. Such dynamics have led to a fundamental shift in assumptions and expectations pertaining to leadership. In a majority of today's organizations, anyone from anywhere at anytime may be called on to think and act like a leader. In essence we now all have the "right," through our actions, to choose to lead.

THE CHALLENGES OF LEADERSHIP

The business evolution just described has left us with three challenges:

1. How can anyone who chooses to lead from anywhere in the organization influence others to perform more effectively and efficiently than he or she (both the "leader" and "follower") thought possible?

2. How can an organization elicit leadership from everyone?
3. How can leaders continue to succeed when the environment and context in which they lead are constantly changing?

Addressing these three challenges requires a certain mindset, awareness, and nimbleness on behalf of the person thinking and acting as the leader. Whether you are considered a professional or nonprofessional, supervisor, manager, or executive, to successfully address these challenges your thoughts, words, and actions must be both planned and purposeful. The most challenging aspect of leadership does not relate to the technical knowledge of your business or functional area; rather, it relates to the roles you must play as a leader and the leadership actions you must take to succeed in the variety of contexts within which you will function throughout your career.

Influence Others to Perform More Effectively and Efficiently

Researchers, writers, and practitioners generally agree that leaders influence others in a positive way by generating new/creative ideas, instilling values, making tough decisions, and by helping other members of the organization do the same. This suggests that, when thinking like a leader, it is important for the manager to:

- Be true to his or her values.
- Generate creative (and useful) ideas.
- Consider the current and future.
- Recognize prevailing and emerging opportunities and threats.
- Effectively communicate actions that will contribute to individual and organizational success.
- Monitor the organization so that he or she can recognize and reinforce good deeds.

Researchers, writers, and practitioners also generally agree that it is equally important for the leader to work with the members of his or her organization so they replicate these actions and, over time, these actions become second nature to them.

Eliciting Leadership from Everyone

Regardless of your position or the role you play within your organization, you must occasionally influence those around you in a way that causes them to perform at a level they otherwise would not have deemed possible. When doing so, regardless of your title or the type of organization you serve, you are in essence functioning as a leader. Again, your challenge here—your goal here—is not to attain technical expertise but to gain a clearer understanding of the roles you must play when as a leader you attempt to influence others and to determine the actions you must take as a leader to be successful in a variety of contexts.

The importance of leadership to organizations is clearly evident in the way countless consulting firms are asked to help public and privately held companies; government agencies; and profit, nonprofit, and not-for-profit institutions develop and execute leadership development strategies and create frameworks that support selection and promotion processes, succession planning, and many other activities.

In the current environment, where it is crucial to elicit such leadership from everyone, it is equally critical to accept that leadership cannot be obtained purely through hiring practices but must be developed within the organization. This need to develop leadership in today's organizations is clearly evident; in 2004, U.S. businesses spent 13 percent ($6.5 billion) of their training budgets on training and developing executives and 25 percent ($12.6 billion) of their training budgets on training and developing exempt managers.[1] Countless workshops and seminars are conducted. Numerous books, videos, DVDs, and other materials are created and distributed each year. All this is done to prepare individuals,—in a variety of positions and playing a variety of roles, to think and act as leaders.

In spite of these statistics, research continues to tell us that people learn most effectively from on-the-job experiences.[2] Thus, to succeed in eliciting leadership from everyone *in* an organization while also succeeding *as* an organization, you as a manager must provide a way for people to focus on the mindset and actions of a leader while performing the functions and duties of their position.

Succeeding as a Leader in a Constantly Changing Environment

The "hero" leader of the past (the one who displayed the most confidence, the one who was the smartest, the one who came across as the most charismatic) no longer will suffice as organizations and the challenges they face become more complex, as change accelerates, and as responsibility for delighting the customer is pushed further down into the organization. Today, individuals throughout the organization (regardless of their title or where they fall within the hierarchy) must periodically wear the badge of leadership. It may be difficult for some followers to let go of the "hero leader" stereotype. It may be equally difficult for managers to change the way they think about leadership and accept that they must act more like a leader. This is especially true if, in their eyes and in the eyes of others, their past actions are what fueled their success.

Within a business environment characterized by high stakeholder (and stockholder) expectations, a demanding marketplace, and increasingly limited resources, however, today's managers must engage each and every member of the organization (and to the extent he or she is able, members of the supply chain and distribution channels) to increasingly contribute to the organization's success by applying their knowledge, skills, and abilities *at* the right time and *in* the most effective and efficient manner.

To contribute to their organization's success, managers might instinctively focus on:

- Developing the best business strategy
- Hiring the best people
- Employing the greatest expertise
- Streamlining business processes
- Squeezing efficiencies out of their organization
- Responding to marketplace demands

Yet, we all have worked in or can name organizations that:

- Develop strong business strategies, but fail to execute them or (as necessary) modify them
- Hire the best people, but can't seem to retain them
- Employ the greatest expertise, but produce inappropriate or low-quality products or provide inadequate or suboptimal services
- Streamline their business processes, but fail to give customers what they want
- Squeeze efficiencies out of their organization, but fail to deliver on their value proposition
- Respond to marketplace demands, but fail to do so in a cost-effective manner

This shines the spotlight on an important issue: to thrive in these turbulent times, when thinking and behaving as a leader, you must constantly keep your eye on multiple and rapidly changing internal and external conditions and, as these conditions change, place more or less emphasis on factors such as business strategy, organizational efficiency, responsiveness to customer requirements, and responsiveness to employee (follower) needs and expectations. We call this the *context of leadership*. Leadership thought, words, and actions must take into account the context within which the organization exists. To doubt this is to ignore countless stories of successful executives who quickly failed after having moved to different organizations or different areas within the same organization.

IMPLICATIONS

Globalization; quality and continuous improvement efforts; new techniques in research, development, manufacturing, and distribution; and many other things impact the organization and the individual. *The manner in which such factors impact the individual depends on whether he or she possesses the mindset of a leader, and the extent to which they impact the organization depends on the organization's leaders.*

As has been suggested, several factors directly contribute to a successful organization. Business strategies must address the current and emerging needs of the marketplace. Major business processes must be effective and efficient. The organization not only must control the quality of its products and services, but it must also strive to improve them. Customer needs and expectations must be solicited, and customers must be given what they want, when the want it, in the way they want it, and at a price they agree with and can afford. *Leadership is typically the driving force behind these factors and conditions being in place.*

To survive in today's turbulent environment, people and organizations must:

- Constantly monitor the context within which they find themselves and respond quickly, when the situation demands it
- Recognize and make sense of complexity and paradoxical situations
- Come up with and be able to execute new ideas relating to:
  - Strategies for addressing the needs and expectations of those for whom they are providing a product or service
  - Functioning or operating in an effective and efficient manner
  - Thinking, behaving, and performing in a way that exemplifies a commitment to quality
  - Not settling for the status quo, but for continuously seeking ways to do things better
  - Delivering on their strategies and value proposition by giving customers what they want, when they want it, in the way they want it, at a price they agree with and can afford
- Constantly send out consistent messages to introduce and reinforce the organization's value proposition and what one must do to successfully deliver on that value proposition

Leadership is typically the driving force behind the organization's being able to deliver on its value proposition. For an organization to truly succeed, it is imperative that managers think and behave as leaders. Managers acting as leaders can:

- Influence others to perform more effectively and efficiently than they thought possible
- Elicit leadership from everyone in the organization
- Continue to succeed, and help others continue to succeed, when the environment in which they lead is constantly changing

Absent leadership, action without meaningful consequence, prevails. Only through effective leadership do organizations and their people achieve success.

THE MANAGER AS LEADER

In our conversations with many leaders, and in our own personal reflections when serving as leaders, we find leaders have several common desires. Most leaders want to:

- Be effective
- Help others
- Accomplish something with and through other people that is bigger than what any single individual can accomplish

We use the remainder of this book to explore the following three concepts we believe will be useful as you (as leader) strive to influence others, elicit leadership from others in a manner that does not distract or remove them from their daily responsibilities, and modify your leadership thoughts, words, and actions to acknowledge and address changing contexts:

1. Successful leaders effectively perform a variety of leadership roles.
2. Successful leaders take leadership *context* into consideration by answering three simple questions that help them determine which leadership roles they should emphasize.
3. Successful leaders focus on what is important each and every day.

Leadership Roles

Our review of leadership literature and analysis of leadership behavior suggest that successful leaders perform the following nine roles:

- Custodial leader
- Trusted leader
- Trusting leader

- Nurturing leader
- Strategic leader
- Supportive leader
- Developmental leader
- Inspiring leader
- Working leader

Chapter 2 describes how we determined the relevance of these roles and how the roles interact. Chapter 3 more fully describes each of the nine roles and representative leadership actions.

Addressing Your Leadership Context

There are six common organizational contexts in which leaders lead. Consider these contexts as the set of expectations held of you as a leader. These contexts might involve your being asked to:

- Launch a new organization
- Take an organization in a new direction from a successful state when people are open to change
- Take an organization in a new direction from a successful state when people are resistant to change
- Take an organization in a new direction from a failed state
- Maintain a current path or state for the organization as the current leader
- Maintain a current path or state for the organization as the new leader

Chapters 4 through 9 help you use an understanding of organizational context to determine which leadership roles you should emphasize by answering three questions every follower has of his or her leader:

1. Why should I follow you?
2. Where are you leading me?
3. How will you help me get there?

Focusing Your Leadership

The rest of this book will help you apply what you learn in the first four chapters and focus in on the leadership actions you need to emphasize on a daily basis. Chapter 10 discusses the skills and competencies you need to exhibit to be successful in the leadership roles. Chapter 11 provides a tool to help you diagnose your leadership context and determine the roles and skills most appropriate for your prevailing context. Chapter 12 presents an on-the-job approach for developing your leadership skills and then using your leadership skills to improve your organization. Chapter 13 includes tools for action planning and Chapter 14 provides sources of additional information.

A Metaphor to Help Guide You

We are not surprised if all of this seems a bit overwhelming. The challenge of presenting a model of leadership comprehensive enough to be useful to managers is to present it in a way that is understandable and immediately applicable (so you can soon go home feeling like you accomplished something without having completely exhausted yourself).

To help overcome this challenge, we ask you to consider a simple metaphor—think of leadership as a light. We realize that as with a flashlight, you cannot shine your light everywhere at once; doing so is impossible, would require too much energy, and would in all likelihood burn out *your* light. Given your current set of circumstances:

- Should you be shining your light into the distance?
- Should you be shining it in front of everyone's feet?
- Do you need to line up everyone behind you as you shine your light forward?
- Do you need to be handing out lights to those standing beside and behind you?

One final word of caution before you proceed. Although we do our best to present a model that allows you, in your role as manager, to act like a leader, do not rely on it to identify the *best* and *only* actions you should take as a leader. To paraphrase Dr. William Sloane Coffin Jr., too many of us use leadership models as a drunk uses a lamppost—for support rather than illumination. If you are to succeed as a leader in today's complex and constantly changing environment, you must choose to use this framework as a source of illumination.

TWO

Background

When we talk to managers, they tell us that the greatest challenge facing organizations today is the pace of change. The world is moving at an accelerated rate. Mergers occur and competitors emerge almost overnight. Customer and constituent expectations change as people become more sophisticated (in part, because of the popularity of the Internet). Economic pressures, driven internally from within the boardroom and externally through greater socioeconomic forces, require managers to do more with less. As the space within which organizations operate changes, so do the needs and expectations of their customers, clients, constituents, and stakeholders both inside and outside of the organization. As needs and expectations change, so must the emphasis and focus of the manager.

Organizations operating within such a complex and rapidly changing environment recognize the importance of leadership. Leadership helps set the stage for success by getting organizations and their people to focus on what's truly important. Leadership helps establish boundaries, empower the workforce, and provide necessary support. Absent leadership, action without meaningful consequence, may prevail. Only through effective leadership do organizations and their people achieve optimal success. How important are good leaders? The stories of Enron, Imclone, and Global Crossing ultimately provide the answer.

The quest for organizations to provide good leadership has led to a large amount of excellent (and, to be honest, some not-so-excellent) information published for leaders. We are familiar with these numerous leadership models. We choose not to duplicate or supplant this work, but to build on it. We have incorporated the tenets of many of these models into our thinking and have attempted to incorporate their principles into our practices. This chapter describes the evolution of the *Contextual Leadership Model* and how it extends the work of many who have developed and shared models that offer specific advice to leaders.

A situation we experienced while working for a Fortune 50 company was the impetus for our investigation into leadership models. We were responsible for the content and delivery of a leadership development program that emphasized a popular leadership model. Our curriculum committee had found this model easy to understand, practical, and applicable. Feedback from participants was consistently positive. Then it was announced that we were merging with another company. Suddenly, the leadership model on which the program was based seemed to offer little useful advice. The reason? Our context had changed.

Therefore we reviewed books, journals, and magazines containing popular leadership models. Our research revealed that leadership advice currently available to managers has several shortcomings:

- Much of it offers great advice but does so by providing a list of leadership principles or actions rather than a comprehensive framework. The weakness here is that the principles and actions may not apply to the context in which the reader finds himself or herself.
- Much of it focuses on a single aspect or area of leadership. The weakness here is that such advice does not address the vast array of expectations that followers have of leaders and is useful only if the particular aspect or area of leadership applies to the reader or is the area in which the reader needs to further develop.
- Much of it describes a comprehensive model of leadership but fails to describe how the model can be applied to different contexts. This leaves the reader with the challenge of determining how to apply the model to his or her specific situation.

We set a goal to create a leadership framework to address these shortcomings. We:

- Decided to develop a framework that:
  - Offers a comprehensive leadership model that addresses the vast array of expectations followers have of their leaders
  - Addresses the variety of contexts that leaders face as they progress through their careers

- Recognized the importance of:
  - Presenting the resulting framework in a way that allows leaders to translate gained knowledge into action
  - Providing the support leaders need to use the framework to focus their leadership in a manner that addresses their current and future contexts

ADDRESSING FOLLOWER EXPECTATIONS

In spite of the seeming prevalence of Enron-type mismanagement, we believe the vast majority of leaders are motivated by the desire to help their organizations and teams succeed. These leaders also work hard to deliver value to everyone who has a stake in the success of the organization, whether it be the customer or shareholder of a public company; the citizen who feels safe and protected as a result of the efforts of our armed services or federal, state, or municipal employees; the member of a religious congregation who enjoys a more worshipful experience in a renovated building; or the many employees who show up to work endeavoring to do a good job in spite of ever-increasing changes that confront them daily.

These leaders thirst for knowledge *and* strive for success. This framework presents information about the expectations followers have of their leaders in a way that is easily understandable and that allows busy leaders to translate this information into action. The Contextual Leadership Model will help leaders acknowledge, respond to, and shape the context within which they lead. In doing so, the leader will be in a better position to:

- *Maintain* the current focus and help the organization leverage previous success and deliver on its value proposition
- *Challenge* the status quo and push forward critical cultural change throughout the organization
- *Recognize* and help the organization capitalize on critical business, market, societal, or industry changes
- *Align* the organization and its people behind a key strategy and help set the stage for its successful execution

THE IMPORTANCE OF CONTEXT

Context is important to every aspect of our lives. Without it, one might step out on a hot, humid morning wearing arctic apparel (not exactly in the wearer's best interest, unless there happens to be a nearby walk-in cooler). Context is important not only to our personal lives but also to our professional lives. Without taking context into consideration, marketers might send messages consumers find irrelevant and uninteresting and thus deem the product or service as being "worthless." With so much to lose, the marketing profession has given decades of study to the issue of context. From lessons learned throughout their industry and from what have become their profession's best practices, marketers now recognize the importance of services, products, messages, and tones having an "affinity" with the assumptions, expectations, and circumstances (the environment) in which they are being marketed. In short, marketers today focus on helping ensure that the products and services being marketed, and the way they are marketed, are contextually relevant to the consumer.

More than 20 years ago, research revealed the importance of context in the one-on-one interactions between leaders and their followers. Situational leadership heightened our awareness of the importance of "matching" leadership styles with development levels. Practitioners, consultants, educators, and researchers have come to recognize a myriad of factors one must consider when attempting to lead people and organizations. These factors include personal preferences, self-motivation levels, levels of competency, self-confidence, and personal commitment. In combination, these factors may inadvertently contribute to a manager being successful in personal interactions with some individuals displaying a certain combination of factors and a dismal failure in personal interactions with other individuals displaying a different combination of factors. Situational leadership offers excellent advice on how to vary one-on-one interactions based on the different factors present within individuals.

In spite of this research, little has been done to explore the different *organizational* requirements that impact the one-to-many interactions (versus one-to-one interactions) a manager has as a leader and how these differing requirements impact his or her ability to successfully lead people. What are you expected to achieve as a leader? Must you lead your organization in a currently established direction? Must you lead your organization in a new direction? Is there resistance to or acceptance of the direction you are leading? Do you have plenty of time or must you quickly move forward? Is the recent past of the organization one of success or of failure? Are you new to the organization, or do you and the people you are leading have a clear understanding of what to expect from each other? Add to this complexity the fact that the external competitive requirements are constantly changing, the capabilities of the organization are constantly changing and, as you go through your career, the answers to the preceding questions are constantly changing—sometimes in the blink of an eye. Failure to understand these contexts and appropriately alter how you focus the performance of your organization through your "one-to-many" interactions is a key reason for many leadership failures. The Contextual Leadership Model will help leaders avoid such failure.

ENHANCING LEADERSHIP FOCUS

To succeed in the milieu of complexity just described, you must constantly monitor follower preferences and capabilities, as well as the current and emerging requirements and capabilities of the organization. The leader with an awareness of the needs and expectations of the followers, as well as an understanding of the pressures being exerted against the organization, is in a much better position to take appropriate action. Unfortunately, although the need to take action may be obvious, the willingness and ability to take such appropriate action are more easily said than done. We typically believe that what has worked for us in the past feels right, normal, and comfortable, and therefore should also work for us now regardless of changing circumstance. Discomfort comes from the ambiguity and uncertainty that accompany new thinking and new behaviors. The Contextual Leadership Model recognizes the importance of:

- Working through the discomfort, to ensure managers' actions are in the best interest of the followers and organization
- Focusing on *what* needs to occur
- Getting *how* it needs to occur right, knowing that simply getting the *what* right as a leader is insufficient

Working through such discomfort and getting the *what* and *how* correct, although challenging in such a complex environment, are possible if one maintains the proper focus.

THE JOURNEY TO CONTEXTUAL LEADERSHIP

You are undoubtedly familiar with the countless number of leadership books currently available. The popularity of these books is no accident; it reflects everyone's desire to enhance their leadership skills so they can excel as a leader. Like us, today's leaders have also become familiar with numerous leadership frameworks, have incorporated key tenets into their thinking, and have attempted to put a multitude of leadership principles into practice.

As we have described previously, the Contextual Leadership Model was not created in a vacuum. Our framework leverages the strength of:

- Existing leadership models that present practical advice
- Leadership models designed, tested, and applied by leaders with whom we have worked
- Various studies on leadership and management and how they defined leadership actions and activities

- Practitioner and industry perspectives of what differentiates leadership and management and what one must do to be effective at either or both
- Landmark research pertaining to talent management, influence and persuasion, and change management

The Contextual Leadership Model benefits from the thought leadership of many (for a partial listing, see Table 2.1).

Table 2.1
Prevailing Leadership Frameworks and Models

Source	Research Base	Findings
Leaders: The Strategies for Taking Charge, Warren Bennis & Burt Nanus[1]	In-depth analyses of 90 top leaders	Strategies that any manager looking to be a leader must know
The Leadership Factor, John P. Kotter[2]	Data from 900 senior executives in 100 American corporations as well as in-depth interviews with 150 top managers in 15 successful companies	Five practices found in firms with better-than-average managements
What Leaders Really Do, John Kotter[3]	Author's experience.	Three activities of management and three activities of leadership
The Leadership Challenge: How to Keep Getting Extraordinary Things Done in Organizations, James M. Kouzes and Barry Z. Posner[4]	Research of 60,000 leaders and constituents	Five fundamental practices of leadership and 10 commitments embodied by the practices
Sir John Browne, CEO, British Petroleum[5]	Personal observations and experience	Four things leaders do
Doug Ford, Executive Vice President, Amoco Corp.[6]	Personal observations and experience.	Three things leaders do
First, Break all the Rules: What the World's Greatest Managers Do Differently, Marcus Buckingham & Curt Coffman[7]	Survey of more than one million employees	12 core elements needed to attract, focus, and keep the most talented employees

**Table 2.1
(continued)**

Source	Research Base	Findings
The Passionate Organization: Igniting the Fire of Employee Commitment, James R. Lucas[8]	Author's experience	Seven steps a leader can take to leave an excellent organizational legacy.
The Passionate Organization: Igniting the Fire of Employee Commitment, James R. Lucas[9]	Author's experience	Seven pillars of spiritual leadership in secular places and three paths spiritual leaders won't take
Leading Change, John P. Kotter[10]	25 years of personal experience	An eight-step process every company must go through to achieve its goal

1. Warren Bennis and Burt Nanus, *Leaders: The Strategies for Taking Charge* (New York: Harper & Row, Publishers, 1985).

2. John P. Kotter, *The Leadership Factor* (New York: The Free Press, 1988).

3. John P. Kotter, "What leaders really do," Harvard Business Review 90 (1990): 103–111.

4. James M. Kouzes and Barry Z. Posner, *The Leadership Challenge: How to Keep Getting Extraordinary Things Done in Organizations* (San Francisco: Jossey-Bass Publishers, 1995).

5. Sir John Browne, author's personal notes, 1998.

6. Doug Ford, personal communication with author, 1998.

7. Marcus Buckingham and Curt Coffman, *First, Break all the Rules: What the World's Greatest Managers Do Differently* (New York: Simon & Schuster, 1999).

8. James R. Lucas, *The Passionate Organization: Igniting the Fire of Employee Commitment* (New York: Amacom, 1999).

9. Ibid.

10. John P. Kotter, *Leading Change* (Boston: Harvard Business School Press, 1996).

To create our framework, we analyzed these and other prevailing leadership frameworks and models and from that analysis uncovered well over 100 specific pieces of advice about leadership. We applied an affinity diagram (a frequently used sorting tool) to this information and nine leadership roles emerged. In combination, these roles address the array of expectations various constituencies have of their leader. We summarize the roles here and describe them in detail in Chapter 3.

The Custodial Leader

Leadership begins and ends with the custodial leader. You must start first with a deeply engrained *desire* to extend your leadership beyond your time—to make certain your actions contribute not only to current success but also to future success. That is the beginning. The end is the sum of all else you do, the results of all your other actions—the *reality* of what you have left behind being either better or worse.

The Trusted Leader

Having others trust you cannot be accomplished through words; it must be accomplished through actions. Be honest, including admitting when you have made mistakes. Keep your promises, be open about your dreams and your fears, and show consistency in your actions. Don't try to motivate others with fear and don't waste time and energy looking for someone to blame.

The Trusting Leader

A key to others trusting you is to show you trust them. Do you make clear the goals and allow others to determine how to reach them? Do you reinforce good performance? Do you treat mistakes and failures as an opportunity to learn? Do you share responsibility? Do you trust others?

The Nurturing Leader

People do not maintain good health by accident and neither do organizations. As a leader you need to know how your organization is doing physically, emotionally, and psychologically. You will at times have to calm fears and at times have to be honest with people about their limitations. You need to build a sense of family and make certain people know that, regardless of what happens, you will remain a "united family."

The Strategic Leader

The strategic leader must maintain both an internal and external view. Externally, you need to understand your industry, your competition, and the reality of doing business in today's tumultuous times. Internally, you must clearly communicate your strategic vision, perhaps involve others in crafting it, but always with a focus on moving forward to achieve it. Strategic leadership not only involves deciding on the desired position of an organization in the competitive environment but also includes actions that make that position a reality.

The Supportive Leader

To be a supportive leader, you must make certain people are getting what they need, when they need it, in a way they can use it. Make certain you have given sufficient time and budget to effectively implement new ideas. Make certain you are consistently communicating key messages to all areas of the organization. Make certain you are doing everything possible to increase everyone's likelihood of achieving success.

The Developmental Leader

The developmental leader gives people a chance to learn, a chance to contribute, and an opportunity for broader experiences and use of their talents. The developmental leader finds out what others have to contribute, solicits input from others, and challenges others to think in creative and innovative ways. The developmental leader gives people the gift of personal growth and, in turn, receives the gift of improved performance.

The Inspiring Leader

There are inspirational speakers and there are inspirational leaders. To inspire people through your leadership, you do not need to dazzle them with your words and the rhythms of your speech—you need to remind them. Remind them why they are part of the organization. Remind them how others have succeeded in similar situations where failure appeared imminent. Remind them what everyone working together can accomplish. That is inspiration through leadership.

The Working Leader

There are times when you must work among your followers, aligning everyone to the common goal, helping people differentiate between crises and mere inconveniences, working among others to solve problems. Find out what others are having difficulty with and what they are finding easy. Measure and communicate progress. Spend time down in the details.

PUTTING IT ALL TOGETHER

The Contextual Leadership Model sensitizes us to the important role context plays in our personal and professional lives and to the importance of our thinking and acting as a contextual leader. We believe (1) there are at least six organizational contexts within which the leader typically must function and (2) the leader—based on follower needs and expectations typically associated with each of the roles—should emphasize one or a combination of the nine leadership roles when working within those contexts. The six contexts are:

- Starting up a new organization
- Taking an organization in a new direction from a successful state when people are open to change
- Taking an organization in a new direction from a successful state when people are resistant to change
- Taking an organization in a new direction from a failed state
- Maintaining a current path or state for the organization as the current leader
- Maintaining a current path or state for the organization as the new leader

This chapter provided background information on contextual leadership. Chapters 3 through 9 provided detailed information you can use to (1) respond appropriately to opportunities to think and act in a way that transforms others and (2) recognize the context within which you are operating and then act by performing one or a combination of the nine leadership roles.

THREE

Responsibilities

In addition to being readers, researchers, and investigators of leadership, we are observers of leadership. We have been leaders and have trained and consulted leaders. More important, we have been followers. As observers of leaders, our experiences show that the art of leadership demands consistency of thought, word, and action. The willingness and ability to influence others carry with it a certain level of responsibility. Each follower must be thought of and treated as an individual, but there are certain expectations and assumptions that most of us have of our leaders. If these assumptions and expectations are not realized in the decisions, words, and actions of the leader, we as followers will do what is required of us in our positions or roles, but we will withhold discretionary effort and, bottom line, not put forth our total effort.

Leaders within one large organization tell us that their followers withhold discretionary effort through "work arounds." Regardless of how sophisticated the organization's performance management system, followers can and will find ways to put forth suboptimal effort and "work around" the desires and expectations of the leader. This is especially true if the leader fails to consistently deliver on the needs and expectations of the followers. To put it simply, if the followers do not accept the leader's words and actions and therefore do not wish to put forth discretionary effort, they may: (1) act as if they are putting forth all the energy they have available while holding back a portion; (2) do what is minimally required, as specified in a contract or position description/specifications; or (3) continue doing what they have always done rather than adopting new or innovative methodologies or practices being "forced" on them by a leader.

Thinking and doing the right things as a leader mean, in part, playing the right role. As discussed our research shows that leaders play nine roles and that they think a certain way and do certain things while emphasizing particular roles. These nine roles fall into three categories: the custodial leader, the key enablers of leadership, and the critical drivers of leadership. Next we describe views and actions of each role in detail through a series of stories and examples. We also highlight specific actions to consider when exercising this role.

THE CUSTODIAL LEADER

Leadership begins and ends with the custodial leader. You must start first with a deeply engrained *desire* to extend your leadership beyond your time—to make certain your actions contribute not only to current success but also to future success. That is the beginning. The end is the sum of all else you do, the results of all your other actions—the *reality* of what you have left behind being either better or worse.

Our friends who captain ships tell us that, during storms, waters of the Great Lakes are some of the most dangerous in the world. For many generations ship captains have relied on the guidance of the lighthouses to lead them from danger toward safer waters. These lights—these custodians of safe passage—are always there in times of need.

The Potawatomi Lighthouse on Rock Island in Wisconsin's Door County was the first federally funded Wisconsin lighthouse built on Lake Michigan. Its first keeper, David Corbin, tended it from 1838 to 1852. Many benefited from his efforts: captains and crews, passengers, merchants shipping their wares, and consumers buying the shipped goods. Corbin was a true custodian of the lighthouse, making certain the light was always shining.

As with Corbin, to be effective in the role of custodial leader, you must yearn to keep the light of leadership shining and work to make sure that when you eventually leave, the light is shining as strongly as, or more strongly than, when you began. Stories of two significantly different leaders, Lord John Browne and Fred Rogers, will help illustrate effectiveness in the role of custodial leader.

Lord John Browne, CEO of BP, is not the typical CEO of an oil and gas giant. His vision for BP—to convert the natural resources of our planet into energy in a sustainable way for the purpose of raising the standard of living of third world countries in a for-profit manner—extends well beyond being profitable.

For his vision, Lord Browne is well respected by a majority of environmentalists. Browne has increased funding to investigate nonpetroleum sources of energy and several years ago broke with the industry by admitting that there was enough evidence to cause concern about CO_2 emissions impacting the climate. As a result, BP leads the industry in voluntarily reducing greenhouse-gas output with their fuels.

Browne also takes steps to make certain the lessons of the past are not lost. Throughout numerous mergers that have occurred under his watchful eye, he has refused to allow the company to slide back to the bloated, centralized structure that almost led to the demise of British Petroleum in 1990.

However, Lord Browne believes his most important responsibility is to develop people for today and the future. Technology to connect people, an organizational structure that allows them to work together, and performance standards that encourage leaders to seek assistance from other leaders all ensure the strengths of today's managers and employees are applied to future challenges and opportunities.

Each and every weekday starting in 1968, Fred ("Mister") Rogers invited us to visit his neighborhood. At the time of his death, *Mister Rogers' Neighborhood* was being broadcast into the homes of millions of young viewers and their families and was the longest running PBS program; however, Mr. Rogers' vision went well beyond entertainment. An ordained minister, he felt television could be used to reach out to young people and give them a solid foundation for a good life. He wasn't satisfied with the short-term goal of entertaining you today; he went for the long-term goal of improving your life.

Mr. Rogers regularly turned down opportunities to commercialize himself and his show. He instead focused on what fueled his success: a message that nurtured and guided the developing personalities of young children. This approach has not only lived beyond Mr. Rogers, but it positioned his company, Family Communications Inc. (FCI), to continue to succeed without him. FCI was recently awarded grants to fund projects for addressing how girls learn math and for training caregivers on how to handle anger in children (for more than 30 years an important theme of *Mr. Rogers' Neighborhood*).

The mindsets and behaviors of Lord Browne and Fred Rogers reflect what we call custodial leadership. In short, when emphasizing the role of custodial leader you:

- Consider the long-term impact of your actions
- Focus on what has fueled past success
- Consider your impact on the environment

- Ensure that key challenges and triumphs are remembered
- Ensure that today's strengths are applied to future challenges and opportunities
- Identify the organization's heroes and ensure that their stories are known by all
- Record the "whys" of decisions so they can be archived for future reference
- Protect what has transcended past generations and must transcend future generations
- Ensure creative and innovative ideas are celebrated, not simply tolerated
- Sometimes step aside as a leader so as not to slow everyone else down

Above all else, you in the role of custodial leader must:

- Strive to sustain the organization for the long term
- Make certain the light of leadership in your organization never burns out
- Ensure a constant flow of leadership talent

Thus, we consider the alpha and omega of leadership to be custodial in nature. Leaders must begin first with a deeply engrained desire to extend their leadership beyond their time. Such leaders take steps to make certain their actions contribute not only to current success but also to future success. That is the alpha. The omega is the sum of all the leader does, the results of all the leader's decisions and actions, ending in the reality that what he or she leaves behind is either better or worse for their having been there.

KEY ENABLERS OF LEADERSHIP

There are many instances of individuals shining as leaders in one organization but encountering insurmountable problems after becoming the leader of another organization. We believe this occurs when leaders fail to establish the key enablers of leadership.

For example, imagine working for an organization for 10 years. What would your reaction be if the organization were to appoint a new leader who immediately declares, "Everything must change!" Our experience suggests that your immediate reaction would be one of shock and that you would be reluctant to trust the new leader. This reaction would be due, in part, to your feeling as though the leader does not trust you (otherwise, he or she would assume you and your colleagues are doing the best job you can), your considering the leader's new position to simply be a stepping stone in his or her career, and your concluding that he or she does not really care about the ultimate success of the organization and its people. Anyone drawing such a conclusion would not likely work very hard to support, contribute to, or advocate the changes such a leader introduces into the organization. This example demonstrates the importance of one's establishing the key enabler roles before attempting to move forward with the critical driver roles. The three key enabler roles of leadership are trusted leader, trusting leader, and nurturing leader.

The Trusted Leader

The trusted leader role is the first of the three key enabler roles we will explore. These roles separately, and in combination, will aid you in getting others to have confidence in your leadership. Helping others gain confidence in you is not accomplished through words; it must be accomplished through actions.

"Why," the young executive asked his mentor, "do some of my employees act in a reserved manner while in the office, but then leave to live stellar lives? For example, a person who is a mediocre performer here was recently recognized as Chicago's 'Citizen of the Year!' How can someone be 'average' at work and then become such an obvious 'star achiever' outside of work?" The mentor smiled at his young protégé. "Tom, I am glad you stopped by today. There is something we need to discuss … a challenge we are going to work together to address. It will not be easy, but I am 100 percent certain it is doable. This challenge has to do with trust. Simply put, during the last several months you have made some decisions and taken certain actions that have caused your employees not to trust you." The young executive peered into his mentor's eyes with disbelief. "My employees don't trust me? I had no idea!" "That's just it, Tom. Folks who do not trust you are not very likely to tell you, are they? Your reaction tells me you realize the importance of your having the trust and respect of your employees. Being trusted by others is something that is earned over time; once lost, it is difficult to regain. Let's roll up our sleeves and decide what we are going to do about this challenge."

The impact of followers not trusting their leader is undeniable. The level of trust people have for their leader impacts the assumptions and expectations they have, inhibits their willingness to share ideas, and decreases their desire to give the extra effort necessary for success in today's business environment. The trust followers have of their leaders instills support and commitment that contribute directly to the success of the organization.

Most people know him simply as "Coach K."[1] Mike Krzyzewski is the coach of the Duke University Blue Devils men's basketball team. Under

Coach K, the Blue Devils have been to the Final Four 10 times and won 3 national titles. His teams over the years have consistently lived up to the highest of self-imposed personal expectations and delivered what Duke's fans *and* faculty members have always expected of them.

Early in his career, Coach K realized that coaches with players who do not trust them fail to achieve the success they and the fans desire. Over time, Coach K has come to think of and treat his team as members of his extended family. As with his own family, Coach K strives to keep his team's interest in mind at all times and as a result deliver what his team members need and expect of him.

The trust Coach K's team has of him is not unfounded. Off the court, he:

- Helps the team establish personal and team goals (academic *and* athletic)
- Provides feedback on each team member's performance, to ensure progress
- Personally—and through a team of assistant coaches and academic assistants—provides encouragement and facilitation to help team members "course correct" when their athletic or academic performance needs to improve

Nor do Coach K's actions on the court ring hollow:

- He calls "time out" at key moments of the game, to give team members an opportunity to assess their play against the game plan and, as necessary, refocus their thinking and energy for the next critical period of time.
- During tournament play, he gives veteran players the space in which to surface as the team's informal leader or "point of inspiration."
- He defines a setback or a loss as an opportunity for players to reflect on what they did right (so they can capitalize on it next time) and where they came up short (so they can personally—and as a team member—prevent it from occurring again).

Being trusted is of the utmost importance as it is key to eliciting from followers optimal effort as well as potentially stellar performance and achievement. Such trust requires a mindset characterized by certain beliefs and understandings formulated over time. When emphasizing the role of trusted leader you:

- Tell the truth, the whole truth, and nothing but the truth
- Lead by example
- Admit your mistakes
- Collaborate with others

- Keep your promises
- Do not expend needless energy blaming others
- Spend time building people up instead of tearing them down
- Do not motivate by fear
- Consider the needs of others first
- Consistently be open and honest, even when it "hurts"
- Ask those closest to you to take the same risks you are asking of others
- Advocate for your people
- Share your fears
- Assess your intentions
- Accurately communicate the opinions of others even when you disagree
- Are consistent in your actions

Whereas the role of the trusted leader suggests how you can gain others' trust, the role of trusting leader describes how you can demonstrate that you trust other people.

The Trusting Leader

How much do you trust others? Do you make clear the goals and allow others to determine how to reach them? Do you reinforce good performance? Do you treat mistakes and failures as an opportunity to learn? Do you share responsibility? Do you trust others?

"Do not be overly concerned, I am 100 percent certain she will succeed." Dave felt very comfortable sharing his feelings, even while peering into the doubting eyes of his fellow executives.

Later, while reflecting on the insinuations and innuendos of the conversation, Dave could not help but wonder what would cause others to expect the worst of a person. On the one hand, it was apparent to Dave that the other executives were suspicious of Barbara's motivation, doubtful of the amount of effort she would put forth, and skeptical of the overall impact of her actions. On the other hand, Dave was confident that she would strive to do all the right things for the right reasons, and that she would ultimately meet or exceed their expectations. Dave's confidence was, in part, based on previous experiences. He had worked with Barbara for the past three years, found that she had performed in a consistent manner, and had always used good judgment (when working alone and when working with others). In addition, he felt deeply about the following principles, allowing them to influence his decisions and behavior when working with the members of his team:

- Relationships with others should be based on mutual respect, caring, and concern.

- Assume that one can rely on, trust, and be comfortable with those with whom you work.
- Strive to work with others in a fair and honest way.
- Assume that others will be supportive and not intentionally do things that are personally damaging or detrimental.
- Never intentionally take advantage of others. You should allow them to do the work you have asked them to do; otherwise, they should be working elsewhere, or you and they should be taking actions to improve.

As Dave gave the conversation additional thought, he realized now that his colleagues did not live by these principles and had, in fact, just as deeply felt opposing views about human nature. Even though their contact with Barbara had been minimal—no, *because* their contact with Barbara had been minimal—they doubted whether Barbara would model their behavior to others and otherwise reinforce their values and principles throughout the organization. Because they didn't know her, they questioned whether Barbara would criticize or sabotage them if/when they make an error or a mistake. And they naturally assumed that Barbara would not give them the benefit of doubt when disagreeing or not understanding their stance on an issue or a decision they make.

As Dave concluded his analysis of the conversation, he sadly shook his head. He realized his fellow executives would never seek out Barbara's advice, would never seriously consider acting on one of her suggestions, would be reluctant to share sensitive or confidential information with her, and would aggressively resist making her aware of thoughts and ideas they had not yet perfected. He slowly shook his head, as he considered the negative impact of their thinking—the benefit that they and the organization would never experience.

The impact of a leader trusting others, or failing to trust others, is difficult to objectively measure; yet, its impact is undeniable. As reflected previously, the level of trust one has for others will undoubtedly impact his or her assumptions and expectations, and in turn his or her decisions and actions. Not trusting others, at times, may be the prudent thing to do. However, when unjustified, resulting doubt and suspicion may be costly to the team and organization in terms of harming relationships, reducing the number of options and creative ideas, and suboptimizing decisions and actions.

The trusting leadership role is most clearly evident when the leader, because of certain underlying assumptions and expectations, is comfortable with others and therefore willingly relies on their contributions, support, and advocacy. More specifically, when you emphasize the role of trusting leader you:

- Allow others to lead
- Give others permission to make mistakes
- Reinforce good performance
- Celebrate the achievement of others
- Allow others to fail even when the risk is great
- Give authority to people to whom you have given responsibility
- Do not punish the bearer of bad news
- Act on others' ideas when appropriate
- Seek ideas from others
- Focus on the goal and let others worry about the how
- Trust what others are saying to you, even when you have doubts
- When appropriate, act on the advice of others, even when you strongly disagree with them
- Recognize that people's fears are their realities
- Trust others enough to share your leadership responsibilities

Consider how you might further shine your light of "trusting leadership." You will likely get better work from others and relieve some of the burden you may be shouldering.

The Nurturing Leader

People do not maintain good health by accident and neither do organizations. As a leader, you need to know how your organization is doing emotionally, psychologically, and physically. When exercising the role of nurturing leader, you will at times have to calm fears and at times have to be honest with people about their limitations. You will need to build a sense of family and make certain that people know that, regardless of what happens, you will remain a "united family."

Who are the individuals who truly inspired you as an adult to go above and beyond and accomplish what you otherwise would not have considered possible? As you reflect on this, consider your experiences in the business world, as well as in volunteer organizations, community efforts, and religious affairs.

Two observations may become glaringly obvious: (1) being inspired to perform at such exceptional levels may have touched you only once or twice throughout your entire adult life, and (2) such instances are as likely to have occurred in settings involving volunteerism as in business settings.

Bill Markham (a professor of sociology) challenged me (BKS) in ways I never thought possible and forced me to look at life, and myself, a bit differently. He was undoubtedly the most challenging professor I ever had. His feedback was the most honest I had ever received, and he let me know in many ways that he sincerely was interested in my growing and developing as a person. He was passionate about my learning rather than my simply preparing for a certain profession or occupation. Not only did Dr. Markham cause me to rethink my career aspirations, he caused me to rethink what I wanted out of life and how I wanted to impact others. When I think back, there were concrete things he did throughout the time we spent together (first, as a classroom professor, then as an advisor to my dissertation committee). Dr. Markham:

- Gave honest and candid feedback to help me understand and address my initial limitations and weaknesses
- Gave feedback in a way that allowed me to recognize, capitalize on, and be proud of the progress I subsequently made
- Focused on my personal learning and development, instead of on my academic performance alone (this ultimately led to marked improvements in my academic performance)
- To the extent he could, eased all of his students into certain assignments so the challenges would not be too great for us to meet.

Dr. Markham's nurturing leadership helped alleviate personal doubt and instill passion, self-confidence, commitment, and perseverance in his students, which in turn allowed him to lead them through their entire academic careers at University of North Carolina at Greensboro.. In organizations, it is exceptionally true that people *will not care how much the leader knows, until they know how much the leader cares.*

Dr. Deborah C. German is the president and CEO of Saint Thomas Hospital in Nashville, Tennessee.[2] She previously served as the Senior Associate Dean for Medical Education at Vanderbilt University School of Medicine. Dr. German is well known for tackling complicated issues head-on and speaking her mind. She is equally well known for making a difference in the lives of the patients, students, associates, and colleagues around her. Although a national figure in medical education, Dr. German is most proud of how she has personally touched the lives of students through serving as a role model and through one-on-one counseling to provide assistance and to make certain they are emotionally and psychologically surviving the rigors of being medical students. She is passionate about what she does, focusing on the immediate needs of others by eliminating obstacles for students and patients alike. Dr. German considers her most important responsibility to be helping others focus their time and energy on the important things in life in medicine, for example, being a healer who tirelessly works on behalf of the patient and the patient's family. Those who work with Dr. German consider her to be extremely demanding, but equally nice to work with *and for.* Her colleagues and associates describe Dr. German as constantly calming people's fears so they can direct their energy to where it is most needed and most likely to be of benefit.

Nurturing leadership is most clearly evident when individual contributors are compelled to exceed in ways and to degrees that they do not initially feel possible. The nurturing leader sets the stage for success through words and action by revealing to the follower how much he or she (as the leader) cares. More specifically, in the role of nurturing leader you:

- Work to establish a sense of "family" within your organization
- Regularly check how everyone is doing emotionally, psychologically, and physically
- Learn from your direct reports, encouraging them to share their skills
- Encourage people around you to more broadly share their skills
- Focus your attention on the immediate needs of the people
- Focus your attention on calming the fears of people
- Strive to understand and reduce the limitations of others
- Spend time helping people get "little doses" of the challenges facing them
- Reassure others that regardless of what happens, "we remain a united family"
- Ensure the voice of the minority is heard and taken into consideration
- Understand the limitations you and your people have
- Focus more on people's development
- Take steps to ensure that people are proud of how they are developing
- Show individuals the progress they are making
- Are honest about people's abilities when you focus on developing people

CRITICAL DRIVERS OF LEADERSHIP

The critical drivers of leadership are the traditional roles that leaders play—crafting strategy, developing people, supporting them in their work, encouraging them to achieve the organization's vision, and getting involved in the details. Which roles you emphasize depend on the context—a context that differs from one organization to another, varies within an organization, and changes over time. There are five such roles: strategic leader, supportive leader, developmental leader, inspiring leader, and working leader.

The Strategic Leader

The strategic leader must maintain both an internal and external view. Externally, you need to understand your industry, your competition, and the reality of doing business in today's tumultuous times. Internally, you must clearly communicate your strategic vision, perhaps involve others in crafting it, but always with a focus on moving forward to achieve it.

Strategic leadership not only involves deciding on the desired position of an organization in the competitive environment, but also includes actions that make that position a reality. In other words it is not simply sufficient to have a competitive vision; one must also be capable of successfully executing that vision.

It was to be a pleasant afternoon hike up the mountain, a chance to look at stars unspoiled by city lights, followed by a leisurely morning walk back to the parking lot. Then bad news came: a cold front would arrive early, temperatures would plummet 40 degrees, and snow would start falling. Options were limited: survive the night with equipment not rated for such weather and then hike down treacherous, snow-covered paths the next morning, or outrun the storm by hiking down risk-laden slopes in the dark using only one flashlight.

Jay hoisted his backpack, grabbed the flashlight, and took off down the trail shouting, "We need to get down tonight. Everyone follow me." The others, panicked looks on their faces, swiftly gathered up their packs and stumbled into a makeshift line behind a rapidly disappearing Jay.

Rewind this scene.

Jay hoisted his backpack, grabbed the flashlight, and huddled with his fellow hikers. He directed his attention to each of his comrades as he said with confidence, "We need to get down tonight. Follow me and stay in a tight group. With only one flashlight, there will be times when only I can see the path. When we get to the treacherous parts, I will step aside and shine the light on the path for each of you to get by. By working together, I am certain we will make it safely off this mountain before the storm hits. Are you ready?"

The replay presents a scenario in which the hikers are more likely to achieve the goal of descending safely to their cars. This scenario also demonstrates the essence of the strategic leader: you as the leader must not only have a vision of where you need to go, but also a vision for how you and your followers will get there.

Meg Whitman, president and CEO of eBay, has consistently played the role of strategic leader.[3] In early 1999, Ms. Whitman recognized the necessity of creating an international expansion strategy for the then four-year-old company. The urgency was real; technology companies were advancing at an accelerated pace, and Internet companies were speeding along even faster. While focusing everyone's attention toward the long-term challenge of creating a global trading platform, Whitman continually emphasized the importance of maintaining the profitability eBay had achieved since its inception.

With her eye on the potential moves of the competition, Whitman knew that all decisions had to be correct and made quickly. She also recognized the importance of involving a broad group of people in crafting the path forward. Whitman did all that she could to ensure active involvement: she polled people at meetings to obtain their thoughts and perspectives before adding hers to the conversation and strove within her leadership team to achieve at least a two-thirds majority vote on important decisions. As a result of Whitman's focus on the long and short term, and the actions she took to make the eBay vision a reality, her company is now recognized for its leading-edge global trading platform.

Robert Horton (CEO of British Petroleum 1990–1992) realized the economic turmoil of the 1970s and 1980s created a need to change BP's structure and work processes. He launched Project 1990 and established important boundaries with the acronym OPEN (Openness to new ideas and ways of working, Personal impact must be understood by everyone, Empowerment, and Networking for the knowledge based organization they desired to become). To accomplish this redesign, Mr. Horton took two unique actions: first, he asked 10 "up and comers" to work together for a year to design the new organization; second, he involved thousands of BP employees in determining how they could personally contribute to the success of the new organization.

Horton's strategy of involving thousands of people in creating the new structure and establishing new work practices has survived two subsequent CEOs and several of the largest mergers in the history of the oil and gas industry.

As Whitman and Horton's actions so strongly reflect, strategic leaders have a dual focus: they work with others to create and communicate a compelling vision (the "where") and then work with them to formulate a path (the "how") to success. When you exercise the role of strategic leader you:

- Keep an eye on the competition
- Learn more about your industry
- Reinvent your industry instead of trying simply to lead it
- Accept input from other sources
- Try to see things from a different perspective
- Share what you see with others
- Involve more people in defining the vision/strategy
- Decide where you are headed
- Focus everyone's attention on where you are going
- Show people the boundaries within which they operate
- Stress the urgent need for people to move forward
- Highlight the advantages to moving forward
- Clearly describe the hazards of the path forward
- Help others focus on the overall mission rather than on the day-to-day challenges and crises

The Supportive Leader

Once the where and the how are determined, one of the things a leader must do is support the efforts of everyone working to achieve the vision. To be a supportive leader, you must make certain people are getting what they need, when they need it, in a way they can use it. This role comes into play when a strategy has been defined and clearly communicated. For successful execution of the strategy, you need to provide the necessary support to members of the organization.

Few organizations have clearer goals than the Boy Scouts and Girl Scouts. The ultimate goal of Eagle Scout or Gold Star is understood even before members join the organization. Progress is unambiguously laid out through a series of ranks and merit badges. The Promise and Law of both organizations define *how* you should work to achieve these goals. And yet, a lot of support is needed along the way: new knowledge, appropriate tools, and constant reinforcement of the scouts. The organizational structure is designed around teams of individuals (including patrols, patrol leaders, and troops) supplying that support.

The example of scouting inspires us to share, through a campfire song, typical actions taken when emphasizing the role of supportive leader. Dim your energy-saving fluorescent bulb to a flicker or lower the shade of your airline window and launch into a rousing rendition of "The Supportive Leader" (sung to the melody, "If You're Happy and You Know It, Clap Your Hands").

If you want to support people share the view.
If you want to support people share the view.
Share your thoughts on what's easy and hard,
Don't hold back a single card.
If you want to support people share the view.

If you want to support people tell them all.
If you want to support people tell them all.
Make sure you tell them all the same,
Communication ain't a game.
If you want to support people tell them all.

If you want to support people set the pace.
If you want to support people set the pace.
Set a pace for them to succeed,
Or give them time to match your speed.
If you want to support people set the pace.

If you want to support people give them time.
If you want to support people give them time.
Give them time to try ideas,
And they'll always try to please ya,
If you want to support people give them time.

If you want to support people link them up.
If you want to support people link them up.
Link them up to work together,
So that tough times they can weather.
If you want to support people link them up.

If you want to support people balance the load.
If you want to support people balance the load.
Balance the load across the team,
Being fair is what it will seem.
If you want to support people balance the load.

If you want to support people get them help.
If you want to support people get them help.
Send the help to where it's needed,
So your folks don't get defeated.
If you want to support people get them help

If you want to support people sacrifice.
If you want to support people sacrifice.
When an extreme crisis occurs,
The first sacrifice should be yours.
If you want to support people sacrifice.

If you want to support people clarify.
If you want to support people clarify.
This will help avoid a big mess,
When you clearly describe success.
If you want to support people clarify.

If you want to support people give them pow'r.
If you want to support people give them pow'r.
Your hiring them means they're not slobs,
So just trust them to do their jobs.
If you want to support people give them pow'r.

For those of you who may be not be familiar with the melody, "If You're Happy and You Know It, Clap Your Hands," let us describe these actions in a more conventional way. In the role of supportive leader, you:

- Provide people with a comprehensive view of the destination and the obstacles and challenges
- Consistently communicate key messages to all areas and levels of the organization
- Set a pace to allow everyone to "keep up"
- Give people sufficient time to try their ideas
- Make certain you have sufficiently budgeted to allow new ideas to be fully and thoroughly implemented
- Make certain that people are linked together in their efforts
- Make certain the workload is balanced for everyone
- Reorganize your teams for more effective performance
- Make certain that people who need extra support get it
- Make certain that you adequately supply people with the tools they need
- Reassure people that they will have access to what they need to succeed
- Personally sacrifice for the "common" good in times of extreme crisis
- Clarify the process for moving forward and ensuring everyone's success
- Empower people to take action

The Working Leader

There are times when you must work among your followers—aligning everyone to the common goal, helping people differentiate between crises and mere inconveniences, and working among others to solve problems. These actions typify the role of the working leader.

During the 1970s, Bob Roseman was an executive of Ketner's Cafeteria. With a 3 percent profit margin, properly handling busloads of vacationers on their way to Florida was for Ketner's the difference between a profitable and a nonprofitable month. This undoubtedly contributed to Bob's willingness to roll up his sleeves and pitch in during times of crisis—with his hands, heart, and mind. Folks still recall how Bob challenged employees to "do the right thing," even with so many hungry people demanding so much. They also remember Bob warning them how easy it is to overcook roast beef if your attention wanders to less import things. Bob was, and still is, a great example of what we call a working leader.

When members of an organization feel overwhelmed or without focus, the organization may not be capitalizing on the working leader role. Such failure frequently equates to suboptimal performance at a personal level and unprofitable performance at an organizational level. Through close proximity to employees and by personally contributing to the business objective, working leaders model appropriate behaviors and help employees understand the difference between crises and minor inconveniences and between achievement and mere action.

"Being on the tightrope is living, everything else is waiting."[4] The Great Wallendas were a family of prominent tightrope aerialists during the1960s and 1970s, and Karl Wallenda was the family's patriarch.[5] Karl not only served as the head of the family; he was the leader of a troupe of tightrope artists that at one time numbered more than a dozen. As the quote demonstrates, to Karl tightrope walking was much more than a means by which to earn a living; it was his true calling. From the time his children were able to walk, they joined him up on the (at first, not very) high wire.

Karl's words and actions showed the aerialists how to focus their attention and energy on the key tasks that would help them achieve their objective—getting safely to the other side. Not only did Karl teach his family how to *become* successful aerialists; he taught them how to *measure* success. They learned that professional tightrope walking required more than entertaining; it meant never bringing harm to the audience. Because of this, family members were taught to never let go of the balance pole because it might hit the wire and be vaulted into the audience causing injuries. He also taught the aerialists the importance of focusing on the right things. Believing that most aerial teams focus too heavily on failure, Karl encouraged his team to embrace—and learn from—their mistakes. Although the Great Wallendas had several accidents (some serious), they were considered to be at the top of their profession for almost two decades.

Until recently, Estee Lauder served as the founder of the cosmetics empire that bears her name.[6] Ms. Lauder considered herself to be a business-savvy woman who worked hand-in-hand with others (relatives, researchers, developers, marketing and sales experts) to make her company the success it is today.

Ms. Lauder entered into business with only two assets: a face cream formula and a willingness to roll up her sleeves and work. She worked first with relatives and then employees to manufacture product and develop and test new formulas. Until she handed the company over to her sons, Ms. Lauder rejected traditional marketing approaches and personally gave hands-on product demonstrations and handed out gift bags to individuals who purchased her company's many labels.

Ms. Lauder was recognized as a "self-made" woman. Although she accepted those kind words, she stated on numerous occasions that her organization did not represent one person's effort. She considered the success of Estee Lauder *the organization* to be due to the contributions of its many employees. Ms. Lauder considered her contributions to be relatively few in number. From the beginning to the end of her career, she worked with others to:

- Focus on a few key elements pertaining to *cosmetics merchandising*
- Monitor, measure, and share information on the *quality* of her products
- Expand thinking as it relates to *creatively selling* cosmetics to women

These three principles are the cornerstones on which the Estee Lauder empire, and the entire cosmetics industry, now rests.

These actions are characteristic of the role of the working leader. This role is most clearly evident when a leader rolls up his or her sleeves and works side-by-side with employees. In summary, in the role of working leader you:

- Help align everyone to the common goal
- Focus on the details
- Monitor, measure, and communicate progress
- Balance "hard" and "soft" measures
- Be measurement driven
- Work among—and with—others to solve problems
- Help people differentiate between crises and mere inconveniences
- Find out what others are having difficulty with and what they are finding easy
- As needed, spend time down in the details
- Manufacture quick victories
- Make certain you adequately supply people with the tools they need
- Remain mentally agile and apply personal creativity to the situation at hand
- Devote time to accurately assess the contributions you make as "Leader"
- Let people know you are open to suggestions and recommendations
- At the end of the day, review today's actions and plan for tomorrow

The Developmental Leader

The developmental leader gives people a chance to learn, a chance to contribute, and an opportunity for broader experiences and use of their talents. The developmental leader finds out what others have to contribute, solicits input from others, and challenges others to think in creative and innovative ways. The developmental leader gives people the gift of personal growth and, in turn, receives the gift of improved performance.

Deborah was still fretting over how to break the news to James. A moment later, James walked into her office with an expectant look on his face. "James," Deborah plunged forward, "I know how much you wanted this promotion. I have to admit that you are highly qualified for the job. But to be candid, we need someone in your position who's just like you, and you haven't groomed anyone in your department to replace you. I am afraid we had to give the VP position to Luis." Not only disappointed and frustrated at not being selected for this once-in-a-lifetime opportunity, James was ashamed that he hadn't worked harder to develop the people around him—those who had reported to him over the past three years.

Thomas walked out of the board of directors meeting shaking his head. He didn't like the answer from the board, but he had to admit they were right. Acquiring a new company requires more than just a strategic fit. You have to have leaders from your company to place in the acquired company to help it learn new operating systems, management norms, and values. Right now Zee Best in the World Inc. just did not have the leadership bench strength to pull people out of their current roles and assign them to new roles within the acquired company. Thomas vowed to refocus his role as CEO to emphasize the development of people; never again would he have to pass over such a great strategic acquisition.

Unfulfilled dreams and missed opportunities are the products of an organization's failure to develop its people (regardless of their roles and responsibilities). More specifically, such failure equates to unfulfilled careers and suboptimized business performance. The leader takes steps, in his or her developmental role, to ensure that individuals or business opportunities are never passed by because of lack of development.

"Fail small" is one of the management slogans at a major food distribution company. Meetings start with everyone sharing a failure. Such acknowledgment yields two results: (1) others learn and therefore are less likely to make the same mistake, and (2) the person who made the mistake receives advice on how to improve. This is one way the company shares lessons learned (successes and failures) and gives its management team the opportunity to contribute expertise they have amassed from other experiences. Also, as the leader of a team where you allow people to share such experiences and advise others, you can find out what people have to contribute while getting a good feel for the capabilities of your group, all while giving your team the opportunity to learn from others' expertise.

Justin Kitch founded Homestead Technologies with a vision quite uncommon for the technology startups of the 1990s.[7] Rather than a quick cash-out on his investment, Kitch aspired to build a company that would continue to thrive 50 years later. To accomplish this, he purposefully established a culture designed to support the company's most valuable resource: its employees.

From its inception, Homestead held annual retreats. This multiday event gave each employee the opportunity to take a high-level look at the company and its direction, thus encouraging everyone to spend a weekend thinking like the CEO. Employees could then examine their own challenges from a different perspective and encourage each other to be more creative and innovative. Started when the company had only 10 employees, these retreats were still occurring five years later when the company employed more than 120 people.

Kitch also incorporated a feedback element in an annual "Company and Management Evaluation Form." The form solicits feedback from all employees and allows leaders (including Kitch) to better understand how effective they are in their particular role within the company. This feedback form also helped introduce and reinforce a key element of the company's culture—allowing team members to help establish goals and plan how those goals can best be met.

These actions are characteristic of the role of developmental leader. Done well, this role ensures that no opportunities, individual and/or business-wide, need be missed for lack of development. In summary, when focusing on the role of developmental leader you must:

- Give people the chance to learn from others' expertise
- In addition to celebrating successes, share "lessons" with others so that they, too, may learn from your experiences
- Find out what people have to contribute
- Give people a chance to discover how to accomplish their objectives
- Solicit input from others
- Give others the opportunity to plot the path forward
- Allow people to contribute the expertise they have collected from other experiences
- Give people an opportunity for broader experiences
- Ask others their perception of what your role should be
- Give people the chance to examine their challenges from a different perspective
- Challenge the group so they think in more creative and innovative ways
- Understand the capabilities of your group

The Inspiring Leader

There are inspirational speakers and there are inspirational leaders. To inspire people through your leadership you don't need to dazzle them with your words and the rhythm of your speech—you need to remind them. Remind them of why they are part of the organization. Remind them of how others have succeeded in similar situations where failure appeared imminent. Remind them of what everyone working together can accomplish. That is inspiration through leadership.

The downpour lasted for hours. Deep in the cavern, the five spelunkers did not notice the water slowly rising. The entrance to the cavern would soon be filled with a four-foot-deep raging torrent of water. When the situation became more apparent, the five had to overcome the fear that naturally surfaces when one experiences imminent danger—without clear thinking and absent a well-thought-out plan, the small team of spelunkers would quickly be in peril.

"Hey gang," Alice said as she slowly directed her helmet lamp beam toward the faces of her four friends, "we've all been in tough situations before. We may not be experts, but we've been doing this long enough to know what *not* to do." She reached out and squeezed Stan's shoulder, "It's obvious that our exit isn't accessible. This domed chamber will give us the safe haven we need until the water subsides or until help arrives. We have drinking water and food for two days, and we know we can stretch that out to five or six days. Between the five of us, we have the clothing we need to protect us from the cold and wetness." With a smile slowly spreading across her face, she said, "We are well equipped for such an occurrence. Let me remind you that if we work together, we will overcome this situation and safely return to our loved ones." Alice held out her arm in the middle of the circle of friends, her fist clinched. With beams of light flooding the center of the circle, each spelunker extended an arm and tapped the other four clinched fists. "Now," Alice stated in a determined tone, "let's put our heads together and decide how to get through this bad situation."

The impact of the role of inspirational leaders is undeniable. In the preceding scenario, such behavior helped to alleviate fear and panic and to instill unity. In organizations, such behavior helps alleviate frustration and feelings of helplessness, and to ensure individual commitment.

His is not a household name. Michael Lee-Chin is the Chairman and CEO of AIC, a firm that has grown from $1 million to almost $15 billion in assets under his leadership.[8] You might consider logarithms and financial formulas key to Lee-Chin's success, but investors and associates disagree. They consider Lee-Chin's inspirational leadership style to be key to his success. For example, he encourages others to do what's right, stressing they do not have to be brilliant tacticians or have powerful intellects to succeed. Rather, Lee-Chin encourages them to adopt a sound decision-making framework and then not allow others to interfere with their decisions.

Lee-Chin modeled such behavior in 1999, as many of his clients switched to high-tech stocks. Recognizing the loss of clients as an opportunity to reassert confidence in his firm, Lee-Chin inspired his remaining clients (and caught the attention of potential clients) by personally investing $100 million in MacKenzie Financial, one of his firm's major holdings. The investment immediately calmed his investors and displayed unyielding confidence to others. Analysts predicting AIC's demise were proven wrong; just over a year later, shares of MacKenzie were valued at twice Lee-Chin's purchase price. Such behavior was also evident in 2003, as Lee-Chin challenged industry trends and continued to donate thousands of computers to public schools and helped students pay for courses. In the world of investment banking, Lee-Chin's leadership style is considered to be truly inspiring. To summarize his personal philosophy, Lee-Chin says, "Our behavior today will be our history tomorrow—we have to make sure it is well written."

The inspiring leadership role is most clearly evident when individual contributors are compelled to exceed in ways and to degrees that they do not initially feel possible. The inspiring leader sets the stage for success by reminding people what they are a part of, how they have succeeded in past situations, and what they can accomplish together. More specifically, in the role of inspiring leader you:

- Show people how close they are to reaching their destination
- Remind people that their destination is better than where they currently are
- Reinforce that people are not alone in the challenges they face and that everyone will share together in the eventual rewards
- Remind people of the dream that started them out on this journey
- Remind people that, by working together, any obstacles will be easily overcome
- Remind people of what they have accomplished so far
- Remind people that they have already overcome much more challenging situations
- Exhibit the confidence and drive needed to inspire others
- Find out what your people do best and link it to the dream
- Give people the opportunity to do what they do best, in pursuit of the dream
- Articulate your dream, along with the dreams of the organization
- Spend time encouraging others

In this section we have described each of the nine leadership roles separately, but leadership challenges are always multifaceted. The skilled leader must be able to emphasize multiple roles at the same time and understand when each role is appropriate. The next section describes six common leadership contexts and provides advice on which roles are most useful for each context.

PART II

Leading in Context

The contextual leadership model sensitizes us to the important role context plays in our professional lives and to the importance of our thinking and acting as a contextual leader. We believe there are six common organizational contexts within which the leader typically must function. Based on follower needs and expectations typically associated with each of the contexts, the leader should emphasize particular leadership roles when working within those contexts.

This part is organized into six chapters and for each context:

- Provides insights into how you might think and act to cause others to go above and beyond what they otherwise might have done
- Describes actions and behaviors you should exhibit when you wish to influence others to accomplish something they otherwise might have considered impossible.
- Shares a case study for how these actions and behaviors occur in actual leadership settings
- Helps you answer the three questions followers have of their leaders

If you are interested in contextual leadership in general, we encourage you to take the time to review all six chapters and think about what you might be asked to do and the leadership roles you might consider playing. If you find yourself functioning within a particular context and have limited time to devote to this part, we encourage you to use the table that follows to select and turn directly to the appropriate chapter that will most likely be of immediate use and benefit to you.

Table II.1
Contexts and Corresponding Sections

If you are asked to...	You may...	Go to the chapter titled...
Start up a new organization, department or functional area	Need the courage, self-confidence, tenacity, and fortitude of Roger Bannister or the countless numbers who built the Great Pyramid	4. Turning on the Light: Pyramids and the Four-Minute Mile
Take an organization in a new direction from a successful state when people are open to change.	Band together with others to continue to survive	5. Sharing the Light: Those Amazing Lemmings
Take an organization in a new direction from a successful state when people are resistant to change	Find people looking at you like Chicken Little	6. Using Your Light to Refocus: Chicken Little
Take an organization in a new direction from a failed state	Find people expecting you to be the knight in shining armor	7. Using Your Light to Redirect: The Plight of the Knight in Shining Armor
Maintain a current path or state as the current leader	Need the strength and persistence of John Henry	8. Using Your Light to Maintain: John Henry Knew What to Do
Maintain a current path or state as the new leader	Feel like an uninvited guest	9. Receiving the Light: The Saga of the Uninvited Guest

FOUR

Turning on the Light: Pyramids and the Four-Minute Mile

Being interested in sports and fascinated with world history, we find lessons to be learned from two seemingly unrelated events: the building of the Great Pyramid and Roger Bannister's breaking the four-minute mile. Both events actually took place: one is thought to have taken more than two decades to complete between 2589–2566 B.C.; the other occurred in 1954 and took less than four minutes to accomplish.

Of the Seven Wonders of the Ancient World, the Great Pyramid is the only one still standing. The Great Pyramid is very impressive. It stands a little over 480 feet tall, measures 756 feet on each side, contains twice as much volume as the Empire State Building, and covers almost 13 acres. We may never actually know how the Great Pyramid was built. Some research suggests it took a couple of decades and the contributions of 100,000 or more slaves working throughout the entire year. Other research suggests it was built over several decades by farmers who were unable to work when the Nile flooded their land between July and November of each year. This research suggests that the Pharaoh required his subjects to work on public building projects in exchange for food and goods during the wet, nonfarming seasons. This much we do know: the Great Pyramid consists of approximately 2,300,000 blocks of stone, each weighing about

2 1/2 tons. With limited surveying knowledge and building equipment compared with today's technology, it is almost perfectly symmetrical (the greatest deviation in the length of the four sides is less than one foot), and for more than 43 centuries it stood as the world's tallest building.

For as long as sporting accomplishments have been recorded, runners throughout the world have striven to run farther and faster. For decades, it was assumed that the fastest a person could run a mile was in just over four minutes. Many "experts" considered the four-minute—and certainly the subfour-minute—mile to exceed human capability. These experts believed the heart might burst or simply stop beating while attempting to supply enough blood to propel a runner at such speed. Such a belief was not held by Roger Bannister of Middlesex, England. At the time an amateur athlete and a medical student at Oxford University, Bannister was an accomplished runner. In 1951, Bannister captured the British title in the mile. For the next three years, although able to devote less than an hour each day to training for the mile, Bannister believed shattering the world record was not only doable but was close at hand. Bannister's confidence was not only fueled by his previous success, personal self-confidence, and unyielding tenacity; he also applied his knowledge of biology and physiology to all preparations for his breaking the "unbreakable" four-minute mile. On May 6, 1954, during a meet held at Oxford, Bannister did the impossible and ran the mile in 3 minutes, 59.4 seconds.

There are several similarities between the building of the Great Pyramid and the breaking of the four-minute mile. The Great Pyramid is an excellent example of perseverance, tenacity, and fortitude applied over time. The Great Pyramid took decades to design and build. The structure required the contributions of from tens of thousands to 100,000 skilled and unskilled laborers. Some estimate that it took just under two weeks to move *each* 2 1/2 ton building block from the quarry, across the Nile, to the top of the Pyramid utilizing massive ramps, levers, and rollers. This marvelous structure was designed before modern-day architecture and is similar to the natural geometry of a mountain.

Bannister's breaking the four-minute mile is a great example of personal commitment and self-confidence applied to a specific objective. Bannister pursued the subfour-minute mile record in defiance of warnings voiced by world-renowned experts. Although pursuing a medical degree at a noteworthy university (which demanded most of his time and energy), Bannister found a way to invest time out of each day to his running. Recognizing that the world record would require tactics not typically used, on the day of the race, Bannister had two other runners set the pace for the first three quarter-mile laps so that he would be in a position to capture the world record during the fourth and final quarter-mile. May 6, 1954 was a very windy day in Oxford. Bannister chose to ignore those who suggested that he abandon, or at least postpone, the world-record attempt because he knew two other runners were closing in on breaking the four-minute mile.

There are two lessons to be learned from the building of the Great Pyramid and the breaking of the four-minute mile. First, the magnitude of one's vision may require the support, contribution, and advocacy of many others. You may have to figuratively (or, as with the Great Pyramid, literally) move mountains. One's vision, without a lot of hard work, tenacity, and perseverance, is not likely to become a reality. The design must be drawn, the roadmap must be put into place, resources must be acquired or dedicated, work must occur, progress must be monitored (as with the four-minute mile, each step of the way), unplanned circumstances and events must be addressed, and in the end (as with the Great Pyramid) the capstone must be put into place. Second, the reasonableness of one's vision may be questioned or challenged. Others may say that the vision is too unrealistic, that it reflects "pie in the sky" thinking. Others may refer to the vision as being a mirage or say that the person proposing the idea is hallucinating. Concerns raised by others and (as with the subfour-minute mile) credible "experts" become mentally and emotionally draining. Not only do they raise doubt within the mind of the person envisioning the future; they also require him or her to respond. At a minimum, such response requires one to call on courage derived from self-reliance and self-confidence. Such response takes time, distracts from potentially more important matters, and adds minutes or hours to an already lengthy work day. As a result, personal commitment to turning a vision into reality, such as starting up a new organization, requires physical stamina, as well as mental and emotional fortitude.

If you are being asked to start up a new organization, this is the section for you. In other words, if you feel you need the courage, self-confidence, tenacity, and fortitude of Roger Bannister or the countless numbers who built the Great Pyramid, read on!

DESCRIPTION OF THE SITUATION

The context addressed in this setting is one in which a leader is asked, or decides, to launch a new organization. In instances where someone is asked to take this newly created leadership role, the person can come from within the broader organization or outside of the organization. The new organization can be a:

- Completely new company
- Stand-alone business within a company

- Governmental agency
- Volunteer organization
- Nonprofit or not-for-profit entity
- Function or department within an organization

In any of these instances, the leader is new to the organization because the organization is new. In this context, if you have been hired or asked by others to lead this new organization, decision makers have already decided that a new enterprise will be established and that it will offer certain products or provide certain services to existing or new constituencies. As the leader of the new organization, you are expected to take this initial thinking to the next level of detail by (1) deciding how the new organization will define success and (2) determining what the new organization must do to attain such success.

If you are living out your dream and starting a new organization, you likely have also made some initial decisions about product or service offerings, how success will be defined, and what the organization must do to achieve this success. Also, if you are starting up your own organization, you may need to follow the advice of your financial backers.

INITIAL FOCUS OF THE LEADER

When starting up a new organization, you are turning on the light of leadership in that organization for the first time. Your initial focus as leader will be on three areas:

- Launching the organization
- Focusing everyone in the direction you are heading
- Gaining the support of others to successfully move in the desired direction

If you are starting up your own organization, you will have already (1) laid out a time schedule for when your organization will be up and running and (2) made decisions about strategies, processes, and technologies that will make your organization a success. If you have been hired or appointed as the leader of a new organization, senior management may communicate their thinking as a simple directive: "We would like you to create a new [organization, department, or functional area] and we would like this entity to be up and running by [x date]." The direction given by senior management may be a little more definitive: "In addition, here are some initial thoughts for you to consider as you take steps to establish new or integrate existing strategies, processes, and technology into the new enterprise."

Regardless of how specific your charge, you as the leader of a new organization must decide, during a brief diagnostic period, where the new organization will venture and how it will successfully arrive at that destination. If this is your own enterprise, you probably did this before you took initial steps to establish your organization. In either case, it is critical that you turn on your leadership light to engage and direct members of the new organization. This assumes that you have employees, associates, or volunteers; it may be that one of your first actions will be to hire, transfer, or otherwise bring needed capabilities into the organization to get the job done.

Once your organization (however small or large) is in place, you must immediately engage your workforce—your followers—so that they embrace the direction of the new organization. Everyone must understand where the new organization is headed and what must occur for it to get there. The start-up phase is an extremely exciting and equally turbulent time. You must help members of the new organization direct their energy where it is needed and help them apply it in a manner that contributes to the organization's success. In short, as the leader of a new venture, you must help your followers quickly understand what they must do to contribute most effectively and efficiently to the organization's start-up; time will not allow suboptimal performance on anyone's part. Decisions must be sound and quickly made, behavior must be appropriate, performance must be effective and efficient, and personal/organizational accomplishment and achievement must occur quickly.

The preceding discussion suggests that the start-up will not be successful unless you attain the support, contribution, and advocacy of many others. In addition, you must take steps to ensure that your actions and the actions of others are likely to yield the needed results: the design must be set, the plan must be drawn, the roadmap must be communicated, needed resources (in terms of funding, human capabilities, and technology) must be acquired, performance must be monitored, and milestones must be achieved. These imperatives require a lot of hard work, tenacity, and perseverance. You will also face unplanned and unforeseen situations, circumstances, and events that undoubtedly will occur, and some will adversely impact your performance and progress, causing you to alter your plan.

If you are starting up your own organization, you will face adversity. Competitors will take steps to put you out of business before you can gain any momentum. Funding sources may dry up. Constituencies will not understand the service you are trying to provide. Customers will not understand that what you are selling is better than other products or services. Breakthrough offerings will be met with confusion as to why they are even necessary.

Likewise, if you are starting an organization within another (a "parent") organization, not everyone will embrace or even accept the new organization, where it is headed, or how it plans to get there. Not only might others question the viability of the new venture, the new venture may divert funding, human resources, or technology from them, and may otherwise require support, contribution, or advocacy on their part. Concerns about the new venture are likely to be voiced, and resistance relating to the start up is likely to play out in a variety of overt and covert ways.

You must respond to such sentiments with decisiveness and clarity; you must address such concern and respond to such adversity without letting it distract you from the multitude of mission-critical actions that must occur during the start-up. You must identify and address barriers and obstacles as they surface while continuing to move forward on the preplanned and preset path. This will be time-consuming and will require you to tap into the courage you possess. In all likelihood it will make for a lengthy work day in which your physical stamina and mental and emotional fortitude will be constantly challenged. As you start up a new organization, keep in mind the courage, self-confidence, tenacity, and fortitude of Roger Bannister and the countless numbers who built the Great Pyramid.

We must share one caveat. The advice we provide in this section pertains to leadership actions. Any start-up is complex, requiring decisions and actions relating to marketing, finance, operations, human resources, and other factors impacting the likelihood of organizational success. This chapter provides advice for you to consider as you use your leadership skills to enable and otherwise supplement or reinforce your technical expertise.

PRIMARY ROLE EMPHASIS

To establish a foundation for your success, four leadership roles are of primary importance:

- Trusted leader
- Nurturing leader
- Strategic leader
- Working leader

Uncertainty abounds in the start up. Where the organization is headed is relatively unknown; it may be that the start-up involves a new product or service never before offered. How the organization will achieve success may be untested: it may involve the design or installation of new technology, the adoption of new business systems or processes, or the utilization of new or innovative manufacturing processes. Barriers and obstacles likely to surface along the way may be totally unknown. How individuals will ultimately contribute to the success of the organization is not truly known, and the likelihood that the leader and followers will achieve 100 percent success or success at the needed levels of effectiveness and efficiency are also unknowns. Again, uncertainty abounds in a start-up.

The leader must overcome the doubt and mistrust naturally associated with such uncertainty. In this context, you must first establish your role of trusted leader to gain people's confidence, so that they are willing to accompany you in the direction the new organization is headed. Once you have adequately established this "enabling" role of trusted leader, you must take steps to create an environment conducive to individuals and their teams maximizing effort, results, and outcomes. Emphasizing the role of nurturing leader will help you calm the fears of people and, to the extent needed and as time permits, focus your attention on their needs and expectations. Once trust has been established and fears addressed, emphasizing the role of strategic leader will help focus everyone's attention on where the organization is headed, resources that will be brought to bear on the challenges and opportunities that lie ahead, and what they can do to personally contribute to the organization's success.

Plans in and of themselves are of limited value; this emphasizes the need for the leader to also function as a working leader. Thinking and acting as a working leader will allow you to work with your followers to solve problems, help reinforce your desire for the people *and* the organization to be successful, and give you insights about personal capabilities and the adequacy of resources your followers have been given. How to apply these roles and suggested actions are described next.

Why Should I Follow You? Trusted Leader and Nurturing Leader

Trusted leader is one of the three enabling roles that lay the foundation for you to be successful in all of the other roles. Members of a new organization face a lot of uncertainty and ambiguity; they are naturally fearful of what might happen. As a result, they are reluctant to trust their leaders. After all, in their minds they are taking a risk in joining this new organization, and it is not the leader who will ensure their personal success. Rather, they will believe in their personal drive, ingenuity, and luck. Instead of trusting the direction and advice of the new leader, members of the organization are likely to rely on the decisions, behaviors, and actions that had contributed to their previous success. The leader must counter this mindset, which, from a certain viewpoint, makes a lot of intuitive sense. To counter such a mindset and to build trust, the leader should consider the appropriateness of the following actions that contribute to establishing the role of the trusted leader:

- Tell the truth, the whole truth, and nothing but the truth.
- Lead by example.

- Admit your mistakes.
- Collaborate with others.
- Keep your promises.
- Do not expend needless energy blaming others.
- Spend time building people up instead of tearing them down.
- Do not motivate by fear.
- Consider the needs of others first.
- Consistently be open and honest, even when it "hurts."
- Ask those closest to you to take the same risks you are asking of others.
- Advocate for your people.
- Share your fears.
- Assess your intentions.
- Accurately communicate the opinions of others even when you disagree.
- Be consistent in your actions.

The role of the trusted leader can also play out in another way. Sometimes a person is *drawn* to a new organization because the mission and vision of the organization tap deeply into his or her personal values or dreams. Typically, the mission and vision have been communicated to the individual by the leader, so if the individual believes the mission and vision, he or she believes the leader. This means that the leader builds trust with the individual as he or she "signs on" to the organization. (This can be contrasted with someone who goes to work one morning to find out that he or she is now part of the newly formed Division X.) Such a scenario is more likely to occur when you, as a leader, are starting up your own organization as opposed to staring an organization within a parent organization. In such a scenario, it is important to protect the trust demonstrated through the individual's joining the organization. This can be done by emphasizing the same actions of the trusted leader in the preceding bulleted list.

After gaining people's confidence so that they are willing to accompany you in the direction the new organization is headed, you must take steps to create an environment conducive to individuals and teams maximizing effort, results, and outcomes. Emphasizing the role of nurturing leader will help you calm the fears of people and, to the extent needed and as time permits, focus your attention on their needs and expectations. It is important to keep in mind that the role of nurturing leader carries with it a double-edge sword. Your emphasis as a nurturing leader is not to give them a false sense of security, a sense that everything will be okay and that things will have a way of working out. Rather, your focus should be to establish an environment that not only sets the stage for, but rather helps propel, magnify, and reinforce, personal and organizational accomplishment and success. As a nurturing leader, you will free up everyone to focus on the important matters (matters that contribute directly to the short- and long-term success of the new enterprise) by focusing on and addressing the matters of importance to individuals (matters which, if inadequately or inappropriately addressed, will distract their focus, hinder their performance, or suboptimize their contribution). Consider the appropriateness of the following actions that contribute to establishing the role of the nurturing leader:

- Work to establish a sense of "family" within your organization.
- Regularly check how everyone is doing emotionally, psychologically, and physically.
- Learn from your direct reports, encouraging them to share their skills.
- Encourage people around you to more broadly share their skills.
- Focus your attention on the immediate needs of the people.
- Focus your attention on calming the fears of people.
- Strive to understand and reduce the limitations of others.
- Reassure others that, regardless of what happens, "we remain a united family."
- Ensure the voice of the minority is heard and taken into consideration.
- Show individuals the progress they are making.
- Be honest about people's abilities when you focus on developing people.

Where Are You Leading Me? Strategic Leader

One way to build trust and calm fears is to help individuals understand where they are headed, how they will get there, how much work will be involved, and what support will be available to them along the way. Such is the intent of the strategic leader. This role is particularly important when working in this context, in that the leader must apply specialized skills and expertise to challenges and opportunities associated with marketing, finance, operations, human resources, and to address obstacles and barriers likely to adversely impact or otherwise impede organizational success. While addressing such issues, it is important that you (1) continue to build trust and calm fears and (2) put forth the same level of effort in helping your followers focus on what is important, so that their focus, effort, and performance contribute directly to the organization's short- and long-term success. To achieve this goal, consider the following actions:

- Learn more about your industry.
- Share what you see with others.

- Accept input from other sources.
- Show people the boundaries within which they operate.
- Focus everyone's attention on where you are going.
- Decide where you are headed.
- Clearly describe the hazards of the path forward.
- Help others focus on the overall mission rather than on the day-to-day challenges and crises.
- Keep an eye on the competition.
- Try to see things from a different perspective.
- Reinvent your industry instead of trying simply to lead it.

How Will You Help Me Get There? Working Leader

As people start moving in the new direction, you will find it valuable to emphasize the role of the working leader. As previously stated, the start-up environment is both exciting and turbulent. Decisions must be correct and made quickly; actions must be effective, efficient, and yield desired results. The working leader, by working hand-in-hand or side-by-side with others, helps the followers understand what it means to make good decisions, exhibit appropriate behaviors, and perform in an exemplary manner in the new organization. He or she demonstrates to others the self-confidence, self-motivation, and competency required for personal and organizational success. More specifically, the working leader helps introduce and reinforce:

- How decisions are to be made and how team members—under actual conditions and circumstances—are to behave and perform
- How disagreement and conflict are to be managed
- What constitutes legitimate barriers and obstacles and what constitutes minor annoyances and distractions
- Time, quality, and cost standards being applied in the new organization
- How members of the new organization are expected to treat customers, clients, and each other
- How to be right, do well, be fair, and be successful in the new organization
- How individuals and teams are expected to respond to challenges and communicate and capitalize on lessons learned and best practices
- What constitutes responsible risk-taking and what constitutes reckless abandon
- Kinds of behavior and levels of performance that will be considered unacceptable, acceptable, or exemplary in the new organization

Not only does the role of the working leader allow you to introduce and reinforce such mission-critical information, it gives you an opportunity to monitor decisions and performance and (1) provide real-time, constructive feedback or (2) step in to course correct, when necessary. Consider the following actions as you emphasize the role of the working leader:

- Help align everyone to the common goal.
- Focus on the details.
- Work among—and with—others to solve problems.
- Monitor, measure, and communicate progress.
- Balance "hard" and "soft" measures.
- Manufacture quick victories.
- Make certain you adequately supply people with the tools they need.
- At the end of the day, review today's actions and plan for tomorrow.
- Remain mentally agile and apply personal creativity to the situation at hand.

SECONDARY ROLE EMPHASIS

No two organizational start-ups are exactly the same. Variations to the start-up scenario may require different nuances in the emphasis of the leadership roles. In some situations a secondary emphasis on the roles of inspiring leader, trusting leader, and supportive leader may prove useful.

Inspiring Leader and Trusting Leader: Solidifying Why I Should Follow You

Secondary emphasis on the roles of inspiring leader and trusting leader may be helpful if uncertainty abounds in your start-up. Uncertainty and the fear it produces are likely if:

- The new organization will be producing a new product or service never before offered.
- The new organization will be designing or installing new technology, adopting new business systems, or processes, or utilizing new or innovative manufacturing processes.
- The new organization faces never-before-experienced barriers and obstacles or faces barriers and obstacles having no known and tested solutions.

- Members do not know what they must do to achieve 100 percent success or if feedback on effectiveness and efficiency will be nonexistent or slow to come.

To give your team members comfort and confidence as they deal with the ambiguity associated with the start-up, consider the following actions as you emphasize the secondary role of inspiring leader:

- Reinforce that people are not alone in the challenges they face and that everyone will share together in the eventual rewards.
- Remind people of the dream that started them out on this journey.
- Remind people that, by working together, any obstacles will be easily overcome.
- Remind people of what they have accomplished so far.
- Exhibit the confidence and drive needed to inspire others.
- Find out what your people do best and link it to the dream.
- Give people the opportunity to do what they do best, in pursuit of the dream.
- Articulate your dream, along with the dreams of the organization.
- Spend time encouraging others.

To give your team the self-assurance to make decisions and to act on your behalf, consider the following actions as you emphasize the secondary role of trusting leader:

- Give others permission to make mistakes.
- Reinforce good performance.
- Celebrate the achievement of others.
- Give authority to people to whom you have given responsibility.
- Do not punish the bearer of bad news.
- Act on others' ideas when appropriate.
- Seek ideas from others.
- Trust what others are saying to you, even when you have doubts.
- When appropriate, act on the advice of others, even when you strongly disagree with them.

Trusting Leader: Solidifying Where You Are Leading Me

The role of the trusting leader can help you solidify the confidence others have in your leadership, but it can also serve another purpose. In some instances, the process of enrolling members in the new organization creates great clarity around the general direction the organization is headed.

When this occurs, and you have been able to hire talented people, you have an opportunity to build momentum around your direction by engaging people in refining the strategies and tactics for achieving your direction. By sharing the responsibility and authority for creating the future path with others, you will undoubtedly positively impact the reliability of their actions. When people help define a path, they leave with more clarity around how to walk down that path. This can greatly facilitate and sometimes accelerate the successful implementation of your strategic direction.

When engaging others in helping refine the direction the organization is headed, consider the following actions of the trusted leader:

- Allow others to lead.
- Give others permission to make mistakes.
- Reinforce good performance.
- Celebrate the achievement of others.
- Give authority to people to whom you have given responsibility.
- Act on others' ideas when appropriate.
- Seek ideas from others.
- Focus on the goal and let others worry about the how.
- When appropriate, act on the advice of others, even when you strongly disagree with them.
- Recognize that people's fears are their realities.
- Trust others enough to share your leadership responsibilities.

Supportive Leader: Solidifying How You Will Help Me Get There

Given the challenges associated with a start-up, it is imperative that you do all that you can to provide people the necessary support to be successful. Individual successes will combine with team successes to yield the success start-up ventures require. As you emphasize the role of the supportive leader, consider the following actions:

- Make certain that people are linked together in their efforts.
- Make certain that people who need extra support get it.
- Reassure people that they will have access to what they need to succeed.
- Provide people with a comprehensive view of the destination and the obstacles and challenges.
- Clarify the process for moving forward and ensuring everyone's success.
- Personally sacrifice for the "common" good in times of extreme crisis.

- Consistently communicate key messages to all areas and levels of the organization.
- Reorganize your teams for more effective performance.

ADDITIONAL ROLES

Certain actions within the roles of custodial and developmental leader may also help you successfully achieve your new direction. Seek out and capitalize on opportunities to display the actions described below while focusing on the primary and secondary roles.

Custodial Leader

- Focus on what has fueled past success.
- Consider the long-term impact of your actions.
- Consider your impact on the environment.
- Ensure that creative and innovative ideas are celebrated, not simply tolerated.
- Ensure key challenges and triumphs are remembered.
- Identify the organization's heroes and ensure that their stories are known by all.
- Record the "whys" of decisions so that they can be archived for future reference.

Developmental Leader

- Find out what people have to contribute.
- Allow people to contribute the expertise they have collected from other experiences.
- Give people the chance to examine their challenges from a different perspective.
- Challenge the group so they think in more creative and innovative ways.
- Understand the capabilities of your group.

WHEN IT'S TIME TO CHANGE
THE LEADERSHIP ROLE EMPHASIS

At some point in the start-up, it becomes obvious that you are making progress and are beginning to achieve the success you desire. You will see that a significant portion of people commit to the direction you are headed, understand what they need to do within their roles to achieve this direction, and begin accomplishing goals you have identified for them. At this point, gain additional momentum for what you are trying to accomplish by shifting the emphasis from the four primary leadership roles toward the roles of trusting leader, supportive leader, developmental leader, and custodial leader.

IN PRACTICE[1]

The Scenario

The Manitowoc Company, Inc. creates engineered products in three business segments: cranes and related products, foodservice equipment, and marine. The Manitowoc Company, Inc. is recognized for manufacturing high-quality, customer-focused products. The company's success and reputation result from its delivering value to its various markets through new product development, globalization, and quality products. In terms of the cranes and related products business segment, The Manitowoc Company, Inc. manufactures high-capacity lattice-boom crawler cranes, tower cranes, mobile telescopic cranes, and boom trucks. Manitowoc Crane's research, development, manufacturing, and marketing efforts have made it one of the world's leading suppliers of heavy commercial construction cranes.

The Manitowoc Crane Group serves contractors specializing in heavy commercial construction, energy exploration, industrial lifting, as well as crane and equipment rentals. Its financials are extremely impressive. In 2004, Crane segment sales grew 30 percent, and operating earnings climbed 133 percent. Its reputation is undeniable. It has:

- A commanding global market share in high-capacity lattice-boom cranes, tower cranes, rough- and all-terrain cranes, truck-mounted cranes, and boom trucks
- The best-recognized brands in the global crane industry

Several factors have contributed to such a widespread reputation:

- The Manitowoc Company, Inc. has a global manufacturing base on three continents.
- High-quality engineering designs, manufacturing processes, and components yield some of the highest resale values in the industry.
- A global leader in product innovation, the Manitowoc Crane Group controls almost 200 patents and 100 trademarks.

Since building its first crane in 1925, The Manitowoc Company, Inc. has become the industry leader in innovation, sales, and performance. Its brands have come to stand out in the marketplace because the company offers its customers the lowest total cost of ownership, improved reliability, greater up-time, and some of the industry's highest resale values; however, the Manitowoc Crane Group is not without its competitors.

To outperform the competition and to maintain its global reputation, the Crane Group recognizes the need to constantly improve the quality of its products and after-sale service. There is a saying within The Manitowoc Company, Inc. that salespeople sell the first crane to a customer, but engineering, manufacturing, and product support lead to that customer's subsequent purchases. The Manitowoc Crane Group therefore stresses the importance of working with customers to maximize the up-time operation of their cranes and to maximize the number of hours they can profitably and reliably use Manitowoc cranes and related products.

Realizing that its competitors were gaining in the areas of cost and quality, the Crane Group decided to emphasize its aftermarket business and take steps to ensure that Manitowoc cranes exceed customer/operator performance, profitability, and reliability expectations. Two years ago, Larry Weyers was appointed Executive Vice President of the Manitowoc Crane Group's product support services. Weyers was asked to create a product support services organization that would serve as a differentiator for the Manitowoc Crane Group—if product specifications, the relationship between the customer and the sales representative, and the price of the product are the same, a customer will select Manitowoc over the competitor because of the value he or she places on the product support services organization. Weyers's objective is to create a product support services organization within the Manitowoc Crane Group that will deliver superior product support *wherever* and *whenever* it's needed.

Leadership Actions: Why Should I Follow You?

Weyers entered into his position with three goals in mind: to create (1) a product support services organization that exceeds the expectations of the company's senior management team, (2) an organization that delivers world-class value to Manitowoc crane customers by providing services that consistently exceed their expectations, and (3) an organization that capitalizes on the knowledge, skills, and abilities of Manitowoc's product support services employees (many with decades of experience with the company) and that contributes to their personal success.

In the limited amount of time he had available, Weyers interviewed support services personnel across the globe to learn as much as he could about them: what motivated them, why they chose to work for the Manitowoc Crane Group, and what they did that gave them a sense of professional accomplishment and personal satisfaction. He also explored how their sense of accomplishment and satisfaction was impacted by (1) what happened to or between them and their co-workers, (2) the manner in which they interacted with their customers, and (3) the extent to which they helped customers address problems and solve underlying root causes.

Weyers also met with key internal stakeholders, including the president and general manager of the Manitowoc Crane Group, the vice president of finance and controller, and the senior vice president of human resources. He used these meetings to determine their perceptions about:

- How after-sale product service might be delivered throughout the global marketplace
- Key events and moments of truth between the Manitowoc Crane Group and crane owners and operators that influenced their decision to come back to Manitowoc for additional purchases
- The relationship between after-sale product service support and the design and manufacturing processes
- How product service support can and should strengthen the Manitowoc brand

He also obtained the stakeholders views on what would need to occur in order for them to consider Manitowoc Crane CARE (what the Manitowoc Crane Group's after-sale product service organization came to be called) an effective and efficient enterprise. These meetings provided the information and data Weyers needed for his subsequent decisions and cued him to actions, behaviors, and accomplishments worthy of reward and recognition. (In hindsight, Weyers acknowledges that he should have spent more time obtaining needed support for his organization from other departments and functional areas within The Manitowoc Company, Inc.)

Throughout these meetings, Weyers shared the following sound bites about Crane CARE:

- It is central to the Crane Group's outperforming its competitors (who are gaining in cost and quality) and maintaining its global reputation.
- It is central to the Crane Group's improving the quality of its products and after-sale service.
- It is central to the Crane Group's working with customers to maximize the up-time operation of their cranes in order for the customers to maximize the number of hours they can profitably and reliably use Manitowoc cranes and related products.
- It is central to the Manitowoc's exceeding crane operator performance, profitability, and reliability expectations.
- It needs to build a team of professionals who not only are interested in helping clients, but who also possess the knowledge, skills, and abilities to do so.

- It needs to survey customers to find out what they value in terms of their relationship with, and the services provided by, the Crane Group.
- It needs to develop a business plan to describe where the new Crane CARE organization is headed, how it will get there, and resources that will allow it to accomplish its mission.

Weyers acknowledged that, although Crane CARE was mission-critical and therefore fully supported by the senior management team, the course ahead would be difficult and not without risks. He attempted to raise everyone's comfort and confidence levels by stressing that: (1) Manitowoc has a tradition of tackling tough problems and overcoming challenges, (2) he will work with key stakeholders to build an organization willing to and capable of attaining its objective, (3) he will work with Crane CARE team members to develop a strategic plan that makes sense and attain resources (facilities, equipment, and supplies) needed for the team to succeed, and (4) to the extent that there is time to do so, he will work with individuals to further refine their skills so that they will likely succeed in the new organization.

While gaining people's confidence so that they were willing to accompany him in the direction the new organization was headed, Weyers attempted to identify factors critical to their success and take steps to capitalize on them (if they were in place) or adopt them (if they were missing). For example, Weyers learned during the initial interviews that each customer previously relied on one or two personally trusted Manitowoc representatives. Although intuitively this seemed to be okay and worthwhile, Weyers realized that it created a situation in which only a select few provided value to customers and thus were the only ones worthy of special recognition. In addition, subsequent research revealed that 27 of these key people were eligible to retire in five years, leaving an unacceptable gap in call center knowledge and customer relations. Therefore he introduced new processes and technology (such as an automated call routing system that does not include individual telephone extensions) that reinforced everyone's contributing to the team effort and gave everyone an opportunity to thrive during customer moments of truth. Weyers also formed rapid-response teams for each of the product lines. These teams provide two important benefits:

- The customer is not transferred from one person to another when attempting to address parts, services, and warranty issues.
- By working together in close proximity, the team members now more easily seek the advice of others (and thus learn more about parts, services, and warranty) and share advice with others (thereby contributing to the individual's, team's, and organization's success).

The Manitowoc Company, Inc. was built in an environment in which everyone thinks of, and treats, each other as members of an extended family. Weyers learned during the initial interviews that the company's recent strides in globalization had created an environment in which employees in one part of the world thought of their counterparts in other regions of the world as regions rather than people. For example, in receiving help from someone from another part of the world, they would say, "I received the information I needed to solve that problem from North America," rather than "I received the information I needed to solve that problem from Janet Smith." Weyers considered this mindset to be counter to the environment that had supported Manitowoc's previous success. Therefore he conducted meetings and held personal conversations designed to help the Crane CARE team learn about team member aspirations, previous accomplishments, personality styles, personal strengths, and potential blind spots. These meetings and conversations reinforced the need for team members to think of, and treat, their colleagues as people. Such actions on Weyers's part not only impacted the effectiveness and efficiency of his organization—by helping team members understand how to more effectively work together to make decisions and solve problems—but also helped Weyers calm fears and build additional trust.

Leadership Actions: Where Are You Leading Me?

Shortly after starting up the Crane CARE organization, Weyers brought his extended management team together to further discuss and decide on:

- Why Crane CARE was established—in terms of vision, mission, and values
- How Crane CARE would add value to The Manitowoc Company and deliver value to its customers—in terms of performance objectives and metrics
- What Crane CARE would put into place to support mission accomplishment and vision attainment—in terms of infrastructure, technology, and business processes

This series of meetings focused, in part, on strategic issues. However, they also focused on concrete issues such as policies that would need to be adopted to ensure consistent pricing and warranty procedures; product and service training being conducted and how it must be enhanced to meet the needs and expectations of crane owners and operators; technical reports and documents currently available and how they must be expanded to address challenges crane owners and operators now face; and a unified support infrastructure and uniform service standards to strengthen customer relationships, enhance responsiveness, and improve the quality and availability of information of importance to crane owners and operators.

These meetings helped Weyers and the Crane CARE management team develop a plan outlining Crane CARE objectives, strategies, major tasks, minor tasks, critical dates, responsible parties, and success measures. In addition, it allowed the management team to (1) decide how Crane CARE will provide continuous service and support throughout the Manitowoc crane's lifecycle and (2) firm up its thinking about how it will exceed customer needs and expectations pertaining to parts, product support, technical documents, technical support, and owner/operator training.

Results of these meetings were consolidated into a comprehensive and detailed report that Weyers used to develop interoffice and intraoffice communiqués. Not only was the information used to apprise The Manitowoc Company, Inc. leadership of Crane CARE plans and progress, but it was used as the basis for information-sharing meetings with functional leaders. (In hindsight, Weyers feels he should have invested additional time stressing and reinforcing to key stakeholders the extent to which their personal support, contribution, and advocacy would impact Crane CARE's success.) Weyers also incorporated information from the report into materials used and distributed during departmental staff meetings. As the audience changed, Weyers altered his core message and terminology to resonate with the participants, answer their questions, and address their concerns.

Leadership Actions: How Will You Help Me Get There?

Weyers believes it is important for the organization be a high-performing team by ensuring, for example, that:

- The personal styles of team members complement each other
- Team members manage disagreement and conflict in an appropriate way
- Team members use management and planning tools to facilitate problem solving and decision making

Because he does not assume individuals will naturally think and act as members of a high-performing team, Weyers stresses the importance of:

- Sharing information with them about high-performing teams
- Investing in assessments, inventories, and other diagnostic tools designed to provide feedback about the extent to which an individual contributes to a high performing team

- Bringing team members together so they can practice functioning as a high-performing team in a relatively safe and controlled environment
- Working with individuals to further develop their personal skills so that they are able to think and act in a way that will contribute to the team functioning as a high-performing team

Weyers also worked with his management team to determine the knowledge, skills, and abilities required of each of the positions within the Crane CARE organization. He considers the time spent on this to be an excellent investment of time, in that it:

- Allows him to speak authoritatively about the decision making, behavior, and performance team members need to exhibit to be successful within Crane CARE
- Helps him work with the corporate Human Resources and Organization Development departments to identify coaching, counseling, and/or training interventions needed to raise the overall performance level of the Crane CARE team
- Gives the management team the information it needs to make sound selection and promotion decisions within the Crane CARE organization

Weyers spends a great deal of his time on the front line. He relocated his office from corporate headquarters to one of the call centers. The time he spends interacting with the rapid response teams greatly benefits him. The insights he gained from his involvement recently led him to place popcorn machines in the call centers and provide free water and sodas to the team members (to help create a more comfortable work environment for team members required to deal with normally unsettling customer service situations). Weyers personally monitors how things are going and shares suggestions and recommendations with those interested in listening. He quickly gives positive feedback when individuals think, behave, and perform in accordance with the new organization's mission, vision, and values.

Not surprisingly, Weyers feels being a best-in-class service provider requires a unique individual—one having just the right combination of passion, enthusiasm, and technical skills. In those few instances where individuals do not wish to think and act in an appropriate manner, Weyers works with them to find a suitable job elsewhere within The Manitowoc Company, Inc. When opportunities are not available internally, Weyers and the Crane CARE managers work together with the individual to identify job opportunities outside the organization.

Believing that role modeling is important, Weyers has invested time and money to allow his team to help develop the Crane CARE strategic plan. Bringing folks from around the world together is expensive; however, Weyers believes that, "These individuals are on the front line of helping a client solve what may be a million dollar problem. How can I ask them to work with a client to solve such a mission-critical problem if I do not trust them enough to help us develop and firm up our strategic plan?" Not only does he feel that such action on his part helps reduce fear, build trust, and instill confidence; he believes that allowing someone to participate in the planning process helps prepare them to implement it upon return to their office.

Weyers must also serve as a Crane CARE product service provider when key customers periodically contact him about a problem they have with a Manitowoc crane or related product. When such calls come in, Weyers's followers are quickly brought into the process. They are thus exposed to how Weyers interacts with key customers, the steps he takes to meet or exceed their expectations, and his willingness to "move mountains" to bring a solution to bear on the problem.

After spending the last two years starting up the Crane CARE organization, Weyers stresses how important it is that a leader functioning in this context:

- Puts forth the effort to gain a better understanding of self, in terms of risk taking, stress tolerance, problem-solving, and decision making
- Takes the time to understand what he or she is hoping to accomplish in terms of the new organization and its team members
- Takes the time to build a team that communicates, makes decisions, solves problems, handles disagreement, and manages conflict in an effective and efficient manner
- Takes the time to ensure that each team member is comfortable with the ambiguity and uncertainty associated with a start-up and that they have the physical and mental fortitude required of someone operating within a start-up environment
- Develops the strategic plan by involving team members in the creation of the plan. Not only will this help reduce fear, build trust, and instill confidence, but also allowing others to contribute to the planning process helps prepare them to implement the resulting plan
- Introduces and reinforces to functional leaders—in different ways, at different times—the importance of their supporting, contributing to, and advocating the new organization
- Provides feedback to functional leaders on the extent to which their support, contribution, and advocacy has impacted the new organization in a favorable manner

DISCUSSION QUESTIONS

1. What actions did Weyers display that typified the roles of trusted leader, nurturing leader, strategic leader, and working leader?
2. How were these roles integrated?
3. Which of the actions described are most valuable to a leader being asked to start up a new organization?

FIVE

Sharing the Light: Those Amazing Lemmings

Many in our generation grew up watching *Walt Disney World* on television and Disney movies in the theaters. During this time the Disney organization developed a reputation for excellent nature documentaries. One of those documentaries, *White Wilderness*, showed lemmings jumping off a cliff into the sea following those ahead of them to their deaths. Lemmings became a symbol of the willingness to unquestioningly, and perhaps unthinkingly, follow someone.

As it turns out, the Disney documentary is somewhat misleading. The lemming population greatly fluctuates in a four-year cycle. In years when the population has exploded, lemmings may move to less populated areas in search of food. During their travels some may accidentally die trying to swim farther than they are capable of or accidentally die falling off a cliff when traversing over unfamiliar terrain. They do so, however, in an attempt to *survive* their harsh conditions.

Lemmings have amazing traits. They live under extremely unforgiving conditions in the High Arctic region. They are active day and night and throughout the winter. To increase their odds for survival, they live under the snow in winter where it is a little bit warmer. They can breed within three weeks of birth. The lemming population periodically dips to extremely low levels—dipping so low as to approach extinction—but they always come back. When the lemming population reaches its peak, lemmings move to less attractive areas in search of adequate food supplies. In other words, lemmings are willing to follow each other not to commit mass suicide, but to survive!

People have amazing traits. They work under extremely unforgiving conditions. They are active day and night to achieve their performance objectives. They hide in the white spaces of the organization where they can increase their odds of survival. They engage others in the organization's goals, quickly breeding support for critical initiatives. In times of downsizing it may feel like the organization is going to become extinct, but those that remain always persevere. When there is the hope of obtaining better results, people typically are willing to follow a leader in a new direction so that the organization can survive.

The mantel of leadership carries with it heavy responsibility. Those who wear it feel the burden of making the right decisions and influencing in the proper manner to achieve the level of success that the organization's stakeholders expect. In some situations, however, that burden can be shared and the light of leadership can be held by others in addition to you. There are situations when members of the organization have a clear understanding that, to remain successful, we must change. In these instances, the sharing of that mantel not only relieves certain leaders of some of the stress they feel, it energizes them. When people understand the challenge and have the skills to address the challenge, who among you would not want to engage them in determining the solution? Who among you would not want to join forces to survive?

So, if you feel like you need to tap into the amazing traits of people to help you determine how to maintain or enhance the success of your organization, this section is for you. If you are being asked to lead an organization in a new direction from a successful state when people are open to change, this section will give you a framework to be successful.

DESCRIPTION OF THE SITUATION

In the context addressed in this setting, the leader takes the organization in a new direction from a successful state and the members of the organization are open to the change. This could involve adopting a new strategy or business model, introducing new technology, and designing or implementing new business processes and initiatives. Realize that being part of an organization that is open to change does not mean you will not face resistance. Resistance always exists when change occurs. It is important to recognize, however, that in this context, resistance typically relates to *how* the new direction will be executed rather than *whether* the change in a particular direction needs to occur. When this is the case, you will find people to be resilient and quite open to change.

INITIAL FOCUS OF THE LEADER

If you are being asked to take an organization in a new direction when people are open to change, you should first determine whether people are aligned around the need to change. Sometimes this initially occurs within a small "inner circle." It could be a lunch group conversation or an after-hours chat where people nod their heads in agreement that yes, there is a better way and if we don't figure out exactly what that way is, we may no longer continue to be successful.

Working *with* and *through* this inner circle you should initially:

- Engage them in helping you determine the new direction
- More broadly communicate the opportunities associated with moving in a new direction and the dangers of remaining on the current path *even though* it led to your present successful state

This context also exists if you lead a successful organization and you have determined that, to continue your success, you now have to take the organization in a new direction. If this is the case, it is possible for you to engage a broad group of people in your organization to work with you to set the new direction or turn over the responsibility for setting that direction over to others. When people help define a path forward, they have more clarity about how to walk down that path. This can greatly facilitate, and sometimes speed up, successful implementation of your new strategic direction.

This sharing of your leadership light can be both frightening and energizing. Showing a trust in others comes easily for some leaders and more difficult for others. But people have amazing traits. Like you, they desire to be successful. And if it is clear to them that a different direction can help the organization continue to survive and thrive, they will walk with you down that path. Four leadership roles will help you start this journey with them.

PRIMARY ROLE EMPHASIS

To engage people in helping you determine the new direction and get others to follow you down this new path, four roles are of primary importance:

- Custodial leader
- Trusting leader
- Strategic leader
- Supportive leader

As you consider a new direction, you must emphasize the role of custodial leader to protect what has contributed to current and prior success. Because you are moving in a new direction from a successful state where people are open to change, you can emphasize the trusting leader role and engage others in designing the new direction. Once you have established this "enabling role," you will be assured the ongoing support you need to achieve your new direction. Emphasizing the role of strategic leader provides the viewpoint you need to plot the new path forward and emphasizing the role of supportive leader helps establish the groundwork for success. How to apply these roles, and suggested actions, are described next.

Why Should I Follow You? Custodial Leader

Your organization has been successful. Certain factors have contributed to its success. For people to respect your leadership, they need to be confident that you respect what has contributed to the current state of success. They also realize that in many situations, lessons for the future can be learned from the past.

At times, to remain successful, you must go down a different path to achieve the same goals. In other words, even if *what* you are trying to accomplish stays the same, external pressures, competitor actions, changing demographics, or new technologies may force you to alter *how* you accomplish it. Understanding the core of what has led to the current successful state, knowing you may need to change direction to continue that success, and keeping an eye on the long-term survival of the organization will be critical. To tap into the successes of the past to maintain or heighten the confidence others have in your ability to lead them in a new direction to a continued successful future, consider the appropriateness of the following actions of the custodial leader:

- Focus on what has fueled past success.
- Consider the long-term impact of your actions.
- Consider your impact on the environment.
- Ensure creative and innovative ideas are celebrated, not simply tolerated.
- Identify the organization's heroes and ensure that their stories are known by all.
- Record the "whys" of decisions so that they can be archived for future reference.
- Ensure that today's strengths are applied to future challenges and opportunities.
- Protect what has transcended past generations and must transcend future generations.

Where Are You Leading Me? Trusting Leader and Strategic Leader

When people understand the need for a new direction and are open to change, you can use their insights, perspectives, and expertise in crafting the new direction. This can be done either with your involvement in the direction setting or your sponsorship and guidance of the direction setting. In both cases there are two leadership roles that will help you be successful: trusting leader and strategic leader.

Use the role of trusting leader to fully engage and support people in setting the new direction. Or, if you feel it is appropriate, you can shift the primary responsibility for developing the new direction to others (see the story of Robert Horton in Chapter 3 as an example of this). In either situation, consider the following actions of the trusting leader:

- Allow others to lead.
- Give others permission to make mistakes.
- Celebrate the achievement of others.
- Give authority to people to whom you have given responsibility.
- Do not punish the bearer of bad news.
- Act on others' ideas when appropriate.
- Seek ideas from others.
- Focus on the goal and let others worry about the how.
- Trust what others are saying to you, even when you have doubts.
- Recognize that people's fears are their realities.
- Trust others enough to share your leadership responsibilities.

Whether or not you are actively involved in crafting the new direction, you still need to provide leadership regarding where the direction should head. Then, once the new direction has been determined, it must be communicated throughout the organization. You play an important role in this communication.

Consider the following actions of the strategic leader as you work to create and communicate the new direction:

- Share what you see with others.
- Accept input from other sources.
- Involve more people in defining the vision/strategy.
- Show people the boundaries within which they operate.
- Highlight the advantages to moving forward.
- Help others focus on the overall mission rather than on the day-to-day challenges and crises.
- Keep an eye on the competition.

- Try to see things from a different perspective.
- Reinvent your industry instead of trying simply to lead it.

How Will You Help Me Get There? Supportive Leader

Once the new direction has been defined and communicated, you must get people to move in that direction. Unlike some of the other contexts that take an organization in a new direction, you will not need to emphasize the role of working leader because the new direction was actually developed with significant involvement of other people in the organization. Having helped design the future, they already understand what the future looks like and what they need to do to successfully move in that direction.

People will need you to support them as they venture down this new path. Here the role of supportive leader will be of utmost importance. Consider the following actions:

- Make certain that people are linked together in their efforts.
- Make certain that people who need extra support get it.
- Reassure people that they will have access to what they need to succeed.
- Set a pace to allow everyone to "keep up."
- Provide people with a comprehensive view of the destination and the obstacles and challenges.
- Clarify the process for moving forward and ensuring everyone's success.
- Personally sacrifice for the "common" good in times of extreme crisis.
- Make certain the workload is balanced for everyone.
- Make certain you have sufficiently budgeted to allow new ideas to be fully and thoroughly implemented.
- Consistently communicate key messages to all areas and levels of the organization.
- Empower people to take action.
- Reorganize your teams for more effective performance.
- Give people sufficient time to try their ideas.

SECONDARY ROLE EMPHASIS

Although important, certain roles may need to receive secondary emphasis when taking an organization in a new direction. In some situations a secondary emphasis on the roles of trusted leader, nurturing leader, and developmental leader may prove useful.

Trusted Leader: Solidifying Why I Should Follow You

The role of the trusted leader can be used to strike the appropriate balance between an organization's maintaining the current path and its responding to unforeseen and unplanned forces. Operating in today's turbulent business environment, leaders recognize that the "space" within which the organization functions must be closely monitored, and the organization's strategic plan (thus, the full gamut of its will and resources) must quickly change to respond to unforeseen and unplanned situations and circumstances. In today's environment, business as usual can quickly become business as unusual. Today's leader must therefore reinforce to his or her followers that if or when the organization's path needs to change, they can have the confidence that the leader will be there to lead them to the new destination. In particular, if you are leading in an extremely volatile environment, seek out opportunities to earn the trust of your people by taking the following actions of the trusted leader:

- Tell the truth, the whole truth, and nothing but the truth.
- Lead by example.
- Admit your mistakes.
- Collaborate with others.
- Keep your promises.
- Spend time building people up instead of tearing them down.
- Consider the needs of others first.
- Consistently be open and honest, even when it "hurts."
- Ask those closest to you to take the same risks you are asking of others.
- Advocate for your people.
- Share your fears.
- Assess your intentions.
- Accurately communicate the opinions of others even when you disagree.
- Be consistent in your actions.

Nurturing Leader and Developmental Leader: Solidifying How You Will Help Me Get There

Whenever you are trying to change the direction of an organization, there is a balancing act between how much pressure to apply to "push" people in the new direction in order to get there as quickly as possible and how gentle to be to make certain you arrive at your new destination with everyone still part of the organization and emotionally and psychologically intact. The role of nurturing leader will allow you to help others get to the new destination when you have the luxury of moving at a pace that lets you bring everyone along with you or when you feel the people in the organization are becoming so stressed about the changes taking place that the success of the organization is threatened. If either of these situations describes your current context, consider the following actions to emphasize the role of the nurturing leader:

- Work to establish a sense of "family" within your organization.
- Regularly check how everyone is doing emotionally, psychologically, and physically.
- Learn from your direct reports, encouraging them to share their skills.
- Spend time helping people get "little doses" of the challenges facing them.
- Ensure the voice of the minority is heard and taken into consideration.
- Strive to understand and reduce the limitations of others.
- Show individuals the progress they are making.
- Be honest about people's abilities when you focus on developing people.

Taking an organization in a new direction can be a great opportunity for developing people—an opportunity that is not always available. One can learn a lot about leadership when trying to change the direction of an organization. If you have the luxury of stretching and testing out the talents of some of the people in your organization, consider the following actions of the developmental leader:

- Give people the chance to learn from others' expertise.
- In addition to celebrating successes, share "lessons" with others so that they, too, may learn from your experiences.
- Find out what people have to contribute.
- Solicit input from others.
- Give others the opportunity to plot the path forward.
- Allow people to contribute the expertise they have collected from other experiences.
- Give people the chance to examine their challenges from a different perspective.
- Challenge the group so that they think in more creative and innovative ways.
- Give people an opportunity for broader experiences.
- Understand the capabilities of your group.

ADDITIONAL ROLES

Certain actions within the roles of working leader and inspiring leader may also help you successfully achieve your new direction. While focusing on the primary and secondary roles, capitalize on opportunities to display these actions:

Working Leader

- Work among—and with—others to solve problems.
- Monitor, measure, and communicate progress.
- Make certain you adequately supply people with the tools they need.
- Let people know you are open to suggestions and recommendations.
- At the end of the day, review today's actions and plan for tomorrow.
- Focus on the details.
- Be measurement driven.
- Balance "hard" and "soft" measures.
- Manufacture quick victories.
- Help align everyone to the common goal.

Inspiring Leader

- Remind people that their destination is better than where they currently are.
- Reinforce that people are not alone in the challenges they face and that everyone will share together in the eventual rewards.
- Remind people that, by working together, any obstacles will be easily overcome.
- Remind people of what they have accomplished so far.
- Remind people that they have already overcome much more challenging situations.
- Exhibit the confidence and drive needed to inspire others.
- Give people the opportunity to do what they do best, in pursuit of the dream.
- Articulate your dream, along with the dreams of the organization.
- Spend time encouraging others.

WHEN IT'S TIME TO CHANGE THE
LEADERSHIP ROLE EMPHASIS

When you have made significant progress toward achieving your new direction, individuals are accomplishing their goals, and everyone is generally moving in the right direction, it is time to think about shifting emphasis in your leadership roles. When shifting emphasis, consider moving:

- Away from the roles of strategic leader and supportive leader (if support networks have been established)
- Toward the roles of nurturing leader, developmental leader, and inspiring leader

WHEN SPEED IS OF THE ESSENCE

When you are leading an organization in a new direction from a successful state, two factors can create urgency for speed. First, urgency can be created when an external event puts your organization at risk. Depending on the type of organization, examples of such an event are:

- An extremely successful move by a competitor
- A change in governmental regulations having a significantly negative impact
- A natural disaster or a catastrophe caused by humans
- The growing instability of a government

Another factor that can create urgency is a compelling opportunity that will be beneficial for your organization.

If your situation requires urgency, you must focus your leadership actions to create the momentum necessary to move the organization more quickly in the new direction. If speed is of the essence, consider adjusting the actions just listed in the following ways.

Primary Role Emphasis

Custodial Leader

- Ensure creative and innovative ideas are adopted, acted on, and to the extent possible duplicated.
- Identify the organization's heroes and ensure that their stories are known by all.
- Stress that the only way for the effort, work, and success of past generations to survive is to work together now to ensure that the organization survives.

Strategic Leader

- Unless fundamental to the new direction you are taking, do not worry about trying to reinvent your industry.

Supportive Leader

- Focus on quickly providing support where it is most needed and will be most evident to customers and to individuals within the organization.

Working Leader

Add working leader as a primary role and focus on the following:

- Work among—and with—others to solve problems.
- Establish short-term objectives and work with others to achieve them.
- Incorporate measurement and communication into all aspects of your day.
- Make certain that people in crucial areas have the tools they need to succeed.
- Constantly apply actions and results against the short-term objectives.
- Help followers focus on those details having the most impact on pressure points.
- Manufacture victories likely to resonate with followers and key stakeholders.
- Remain healthy and mentally agile.

Secondary Role Emphasis

Nurturing Leader

- Don't worry about regularly checking how everyone is doing emotionally, psychologically, and physically—you don't have the time.

Developmental Leader

- As quickly as possible, find out what people have to contribute.
- Emphasize the importance of people contributing expertise from other experiences.
- Challenge the group so they think in more creative and innovative ways.
- Understand the capabilities of your group.

IN PRACTICE[1]

The Scenario

The U.S. Navy is unquestionably the best navy in the world and for decades has dominated the seas. There are many factors contributing to the dominance of the U.S. Navy. One factor is the shore infrastructure supporting the warfighter.

The Navy Shore Establishment is responsible for the care and custody of the navy's shore infrastructure. The breadth of their responsibilities becomes apparent when you consider that the typical navy installation is comparable to an average U.S. city. A navy installation typically consists of streets, utility systems, offices, warehouses, hospitals, commercial buildings, schools, child care centers, industrial facilities, and family housing. In addition, the installation may also include the infrastructure to support air and/or port operations, runways, taxiways, control towers, navigation aids, piers, quays, and numerous other associated structures. The Navy Shore Establishment is responsible not only for contributing to the navy's military readiness, but also for helping enhance the quality of life of uniformed and civilian personnel (and in many cases, their families).

The Navy Shore Establishment contributes to the warfighter's mission readiness through shore infrastructure planning, design, construction, sustainment, restoration, modernization, and demolition, and is responsible for improving readiness by:

- Identifying and fulfilling shore facility requirements
- Improving the accuracy of facility condition assessments
- Improving the accuracy of cost projections and forecasts
- Effectively and efficiently using facility management resources
- Transforming facility management information technology tools into enterprise solutions for the navy

Government mandates require that all military support functions become more efficient. Support elements within the navy have been tasked to optimize Congress's investments, be more accountable for how money is spent, be able to tie value to their budgetary requests for money, and allow the savings they generate to be reinvested to make the warfighter more effective, all while sustaining core capabilities.

The government mandates are impacting almost every aspect of the organization, including its structure, workforce, processes, and technology.

The challenge for the Navy's Shore Establishment professionals is balance. They must balance the navy's short-term needs with its long-term needs, and they must balance the needs of the facilities that support the warfighter with the needs of the warfighter. One process that has inhibited their ability to effectively balance these needs was the process used to assess facility condition.

Traditional navy facility condition assessments require, by policy and regulation, that every asset be physically inspected on a calendar-driven frequency regardless of the asset's age or condition. This is not only an expensive process, but one that no longer delivers information consistently or timely enough for planning and the decisions necessary to ensure adequate facility readiness to support the warfighter. Evidence for the ineffectiveness of this process can be found in customer feedback, data from U.S. Government Accountability Office (GAO), and from U.S. Navy audit reports.

Members of the Navy Shore Establishment community take their stewardship responsibility seriously. They also take seriously the challenge to maintain or improve the quality of their services while working to relate asset condition to warfighter readiness. In an era characterized by increasing tempo of operations and declining resources, developing processes to ensure mission critical assets are properly maintained and ready to perform when needed is vital, not only for supporting the warfighter but also for optimizing taxpayers' investment.

In 2003, a core group of facility professionals within the Navy Shore Establishment led by Roy Morris recognized the need to improve the facility condition assessment process. The development and implementation of their vision became their passion.

Leadership Actions: Why Should I Follow You?

The core group, driven by a common vision for an improved facility condition assessment process, began sharing their thoughts. They quickly agreed that the traditional process was:

- 50 years old and strongly institutionalized
- Too expensive
- Too subjective and no longer providing credible data for decision making
- Not standardized across navy regions
- Criticized and discredited in recent GAO and navy audits

With the traditional facility condition assessment process not meeting the needs of their clients, this informal group began sharing their ideas on cocktail napkins, sending each other e-mails, and creating awareness within the facilities management community for the need to change. They shared their ideas with their clients and experienced positive reactions. They began to be referred to, however, as rogues for their audacity to suggest, even recommend, substantive changes in an institutionalized process, with which the facilities management community at large was comfortable. To continue, they needed senior navy sponsorship to champion their efforts.

It was extremely difficult, however, to get the senior leadership to sponsor the initiative, because the navy was undergoing significant organizational changes affecting asset control and maintenance responsibilities.

Nonetheless, the group continued to work the issue, and they were finally given an opportunity to brief navy leadership. The briefing was a success and they obtained sponsorship. An initial charter was written, the vision was put to paper, and the group was formalized as the Facility Condition Assessment Program (FCAP) Working Group.

The FCAP Working Group understood the process they wanted to improve, and they had a high-level concept of what the new process should look like. They now had a sponsor, something critical to the success of *any* navy initiative. They had gained sufficient support from senior leadership and from their clients, all agreeing the initiative was in the best interest of the navy, facilities stewardship, and the short- and long-term needs of the warfighters. It was now time to get more specific about where this vision would take everyone, considering the current "as-is" process and the notional "to-be" process.

Leadership Actions: Where Are You Leading Me?

To continue focusing thoughts on the new direction, the FCAP Working Group sponsored industry trade meetings, which allowed industry leaders in facility condition assessment to display and share information about emerging tools and technologies. These meetings became a two-way exchange of information where the FCAP Working Group shared data on the navy's current process, its problems including criticisms from the GAO and navy audits, and thoughts on the direction they had charted. These meetings triggered additional ideas and technical requirements that an electronic tool should meet. The FCAP Working Group continued to communicate progress to their sponsor who in turn communicated with other navy leadership.

Eventually, the FCAP Working Group was ready to ask for the funding needed to turn their vision into a reality. The group realized that a strong Business Case Analysis (BCA) was key to obtaining the necessary funding to continue development of the "to-be" process and implement it and the enabling electronic assessment tool across the navy. A contractor was hired to facilitate the FCAP Working Group in developing the BCA. The FCAP Working Group was also expanded to include regional and installation representatives well versed in the traditional process. These subject matter experts were needed to assist the FCAP Working Group in integrating the new process into facilities business activities and implementing an electronic assessment tool in an ever-changing information technology environment. The initial core group wanted to make certain that, whatever the final solution, it would be perceived as a navy-wide vision, not as the vision of a small group of passionate people. During these meetings, the expanded FCAP Working Group clarified the:

- Cost of the current process
- Requirements of the new process
- Projected cost savings

The BCA demonstrated that a standardized facilities assessment process based on sound engineering principles and emerging industry technologies could reduce the current inspection costs by 50 percent, while providing consistent, auditable, and timely facility condition information. Also, the new process takes the navy from a backward-looking inspection process, where every deficiency is considered to be actionable, to a forward-looking process that uses lifecycle engineering and forecasts work requirements for appropriate management action. Senior leadership agreed with the findings of the FCAP Working Group's BCA and approved funding for navy-wide implementation and the acquisition of an enabling electronic tool. In addition, senior leadership saw the need to use change management techniques to help achieve success with the overall initiative. After a competitive solicitation and an exhaustive selection process, a contract was awarded for an electronic tool that met the navy's technical specifications and professional services. A pivotal selection factor was significant experience in change and transition management.

Leadership Actions: How Will You Help Me Get There?

Although the project had been endorsed and funded, there were still many impediments to success:

- The current process was deeply ingrained in a military and government culture that was resistant to change.
- Numerous locations having their own variation of facilities condition assessment processes would naturally resist a more standardized process.
- Regions located in other parts of the world had country-specific requirements that needed to be accommodated.
- Leadership within the navy, by design, frequently changes; this can result in a new leader ending initiatives started by his or her predecessor.

To accomplish wide-scale change in such a challenging environment, the FCAP Working Group recognized the need for an infrastructure to support the initiative. To make certain the initiative continued down a path to where it met the needs of navy users and decision makers at all levels, the FCAP Working Group transformed into the Government Implementation Team, and Morris was designated the project manager for the implementation effort.

A kick-off meeting marked the start of the project effort. In attendance at the kick-off were navy senior leadership and the funding sponsor. More than 60 people attended the kick-off meeting representing all navy regions worldwide, as well as other interested organizations (stakeholders) and representatives from the five companies comprising the vendor team. A series of process reengineering sessions allowed many of the same individuals that attended the kick-off meeting to be involved in developing the "as-is" and "to-be" processes. In all, 63 people attended the first day of the initial process reengineering session where the history-to-date and goals of the project were shared.

The reengineering sessions provided an opportunity for a broad cross section from the Navy Shore Establishment community to offer their input for describing the current facilities condition assessment process and designing the future process. Such a large group presented a challenge (described by participants as "herding cats"), but responses to an end-of-meeting survey indicated the participants solidly agreed that attending the meeting was a valuable investment of their time and that representation of various groups from around the world was important in achieving the goals of the meeting. Survey feedback also revealed that the Government Implementation Team was doing a good job of soliciting *and listening* to the input of their various stakeholder groups. The effort was off to a good start!

The facility assessment improvement initiative continues to move forward. It has already reached several noteworthy milestones. Perhaps the most visible and important is that senior leadership has voiced strong support for this initiative and the benefits it will produce. These were other impressive milestones:

- Facilities management leadership from throughout the world has voiced an understanding of the intent and goals of the initiative and has pledged strong regional support.
- Conceptual information about the initiative has been vetted throughout the facilities management organization (including being described in various milestone schools); while everyone within the facilities management community may not know the specifics, they do know that change is on the horizon and that this change will be in their and the navy's best interest.
- Dozens of individuals, representing various stakeholder groups and global geographic regions, have participated in the initiative and have helped it achieve interim objectives; feedback suggests this group will serve as future advocates.

From the initial core group of rogues to the expanded FCAP Working Group and the Government Implementation Team, the navy-wide Shore Establishment community now considers the condition assessment initiative to be on a trajectory of success. The process that the initiative will follow moving forward was designed to continue to solicit input from, and provide support to, the entire facilities management community. After the new process is designed, the next step will be to prototype the process in a nonproduction setting using the selected technology. After the successful completion of the prototype stage, the process will be piloted in a production setting at two regions where more input will be gathered and acted on. New skills will be defined and communicated, training plans will be developed and executed, stakeholders will be kept updated, and those involved in implementing the new process will be informed and supported as the roll-out of the new process and enabling technology continues around the world.

The "rogues" offer the following advice to people trying to lead in similar contexts:

- Don't wait for senior management to ask you to solve a problem; convince them to let you solve it.
- Make certain the problem you are addressing is something that excites a passion in you.
- Investigate the problem and potential solutions, involve other people in discussions about the problem and solution, map out potential paths forward, determine cost savings or return-on-investment, and then go to senior management to solicit their support.
- Invite a lot of people to participate.
- Find champions to support you.
- Communicate often and do not forget to communicate to new stakeholders as the people in the positions change.
- Keep the "wolves off the backs" of your team so that they can devote the time and effort to successfully move the organization in a new direction.

DISCUSSION QUESTIONS

1. What actions did the core group display that typified the roles of custodial leader, trusting leader, strategic leader, and supportive leader?
2. How were these roles integrated?
3. Which of the actions are most valuable to a leader being asked to lead an organization in a new direction from a successful state when people are open to change?

SIX

Using Your Light to Refocus: Chicken Little

In childhood, we grew up learning two versions of the Chicken Little story. One version was somewhat benign. Chicken Little was in the woods when an acorn fell on her. She headed off to warn the king that the sky was falling. Along the way she attracted a number of followers that believed the sky was falling because Chicken Little said it was. When they finally reached the king, the king found the acorn in her feathers and told everyone not to worry; the sky was not falling; it was only an acorn. This version ended with everyone having a good laugh.

In the more ominous version, Chicken Little still draws her collection of believers on the way to the king, but runs into Foxy Woxy who knows a shortcut to the castle. Unfortunately, the shortcut actually leads to Foxy Woxy's den and Chicken Little, Henny Penny, and the others are never heard from again.

There are two lessons to be learned from this story. First, everyone has experienced a personal version of the Chicken Little story. Someone has come running along saying something ominous will soon happen and that we must prepare to deal with it—only to discover that the danger isn't real. This makes the average person somewhat cautious and reluctant to move when things look fine to them and someone comes along shouting that danger is out there and everyone needs to prepare for it.

Second, every organization has a Foxy Woxy (often more than one). This is the person who listens carefully to you, agrees wholeheartedly with you, offers assistance, and then makes certain you are never heard from again.

If you feel like you are being asked to lead in a new direction and people are comfortable with the success they have had and are resistant to change, this is the chapter for you. In other words, if people are viewing you like you are Chicken Little, read on!

DESCRIPTION OF THE SITUATION

The context addressed in this chapter is one of the most common: it is a setting in which the leader needs to take the organization in a new direction from a successful state, and the members of the organization are resistant to the change. This could involve adopting a new strategy, introducing new technology, and designing or implementing new business processes and initiatives.

Current success can be one of the biggest impediments to future success. The stories of companies such as IBM and AT&T are well known. IBM ran into problems in the 1990s because, confident in their share of the mainframe computer market, they failed to anticipate the impact of the personal computer market. AT&T was eventually overshadowed by the Baby Bells it spun off (and later purchased by one of them!) due in part to its confidence that it possessed the best telephone network in the world. Because of the success of the organization, the challenge you have is to use the light of your leadership to help people refocus their attention. They tend to be blinded by their success, and they need to be shown that maintaining that success requires them to focus on external factors and challenges and be responsive to those that will confront them.

Many organizations must move in a different direction to maintain their success. This alteration might be minor for the organization, but major for a particular department. For example, a manufacturing company that has performed well for a number of years might realize that to continue to compete, it must drastically revamp its operations department. A change in path can also impact the direction of an entire company. Motorola is an example of a company who, over the years, has reinvented itself as it moved from automobile radios to televisions to semiconductors to cellular phones.

This section addresses situations in which you must lead an organization in a new direction from a successful state while experiencing resistance.

INITIAL FOCUS OF THE LEADER

If you are trying to change the direction of a previously successful organization, you must initially focus your leadership on three goals:

- Ensuring there is a solid and clear vision for where the organization needs to go (you may have already been handed this vision)
- Communicating this vision
- Getting everyone to move in the new direction

As you work to accomplish these goals, it will be important to remember the lessons from Chicken Little. Many people will have previously heard and responded to the "siren call for change" only to see it fail. As a result, they will be reluctant to believe you. Remember that Chicken Little "felt" the sky falling, but only described it to others. To overcome this reluctance to change, you will have to get others to recognize (see and feel) the need for this change and then work with them to clarify what they need to do to move in this new direction—all while avoiding Foxy Woxy. Four of the leadership roles will help you accomplish this goal.

PRIMARY ROLE EMPHASIS

To redirect the momentum of the organization and retain a critical mass of followers, four roles are of primary importance:

- Trusted leader
- Strategic leader
- Supportive leader
- Working leader

The change in emphasis and direction you are trying to instill will create doubt concerning the consistency of your actions and behavior. People will wonder why you don't believe they are successful and why you don't think they are good enough to continue to succeed. You must therefore initially establish (if you are a new leader to the group) or reinforce (if you are their existing leader) your role of trusted leader. Once you adequately establish or reinforce this "enabling" role, you will have greatly increased the likelihood that you will have the ongoing support you need to achieve the new direction. Getting people to trust you is crucial to your being able to emphasize the three other primary leadership roles.

Emphasizing the role of strategic leader gives you the viewpoint you need to plot the new path forward and communicate this path. Once people—regardless of the number, even a few—begin to understand the new direction, you will need to show them what to do to start working toward achieving this new direction (working leader) and support them in their efforts to do this (supportive leader). How to apply these roles, and suggested actions, are described next.

Why Should I Follow You? Trusted Leader

Trusted leader is one of the three enabling roles that lay the foundation for you to be successful in all of the other roles. If you are trying to take an organization in a new direction and are experiencing resistance to change, the resistance requires that you initially emphasize the role of the trusted leader, rather than the roles of trusting leader or nurturing leader. You may not able to fully trust others because they don't yet recognize the need for change and therefore in all likelihood believe they must continue doing the same thing the same way. After all, this is what led to the success they have previously experienced. Also, you must keep in mind there will be Foxy Woxies out there waiting for the right opportunity to make certain your change fails.

When you are attempting to change the direction of an organization, it is critical that you work to establish a sense of urgency. This need for urgency requires you to not place initial emphasis on the nurturing leader role.

We believe the absence of the enabling role of trusted leader causes many excellent leaders joining a successful organization and attempting to change its direction to fail. For a moment, put yourself in the role of follower. You are working in a successful organization. You are both pleased with and proud of what you have accomplished. Enter the new leader. The new leader starts out by saying there is trouble on the horizon. You may hear phrases such as, "You need to change. If you don't change you will not be able to compete much longer. Here is the strategy that will 'save' us."

As a follower, think about your reactions to this. Is it one of wholehearted support and a willingness to give exceptional effort to achieving the new strategy? Or, are you more likely to think, "Who is this person to come in and threaten us with all of these things? How can I be sure that we need to change and how can I be confident that this new path is the right one? How can I trust this new leader?"

As you work to establish your role as a trusted leader, consider the appropriateness of the following actions that contribute to establishing this role:

- Tell the truth, the whole truth, and nothing but the truth.
- Lead by example.
- Admit your mistakes.
- Collaborate with others.
- Keep your promises.
- Do not expend needless energy blaming others.
- Spend time building people up instead of tearing them down.
- Do not motivate by fear.
- Consider the needs of others first.
- Consistently be open and honest, even when it "hurts."
- Ask those closest to you to take the same risks you are asking of others.
- Advocate for your people.
- Share your fears.
- Assess your intentions.
- Accurately communicate the opinions of others even when you disagree.
- Be consistent in your actions.

Where Are You Leading Me? Strategic Leader

Once you have gained people's trust (or as you work to gain it), you must establish and communicate the new direction. We do not try to describe here the technical aspects of developing a winning strategy; that is a book in itself. What we try to do here is describe for you the leadership actions that support establishing and communicating a new direction that will help refocus people on what they need to do to continue to be successful.

If you have not yet determined the new direction, consider the appropriateness of the following actions of the strategic leader:

- Learn more about your industry.
- Try to see things from a different perspective.
- Accept input from other sources.
- Keep an eye on the competition.
- Reinvent your industry instead of trying simply to lead it.
- Share what you see with others.

Once the new direction is decided on, you must work hard to get people to recognize the need for changing to the new direction. Use the trust you have earned to help others realize that the need to move in this direction is real, even if they do not personally see or feel it. This will help them refocus their attention toward external factors and challenges. To achieve this, consider the following actions of the strategic leader:

- Share what you see with others.
- Focus everyone's attention on where you are going.
- Stress the urgent need for people to move forward.
- Try to see things from a different perspective.
- Help others focus on the overall mission rather than on the day-to-day challenges and crises.

How Will You Help Me Get There? Working Leader and Supportive Leader

When people have started to trust you and you have identified and started communicating a clearly defined new direction, you then need to engage people to work toward the new direction. This is accomplished by emphasizing the role of the working leader. When heading in a new direction, it is frequently unclear to people how to get started. Use the role of the working leader to refocus people on how their work needs to be done, clarify for them how they need to work differently, and let them know if they are accomplishing things in the appropriate manner and if their efforts are achieving the desired results. Consider the following actions as you emphasize the role of the working leader:

- Help align everyone to the common goal.
- Focus on the details.
- Work among—and with—others to solve problems.
- Monitor, measure, and communicate progress.
- Balance "hard" and "soft" measures.
- Manufacture quick victories.
- Make certain you adequately supply people with the tools they need.
- At the end of the day, review today's actions and plan for tomorrow.
- Remain mentally agile and apply personal creativity to the situation at hand.

When you start asking people to work differently than they have in the past, it is important for them to succeed. If they do succeed, you are ultimately successful in taking the organization in a new direction. If they don't succeed, your new direction becomes far more difficult to achieve, yields suboptimal results, or even ends in failure. That is why it is crucial to support people in working to achieve the new direction. As you emphasize the role of the supportive leader, consider the following actions:

- Make certain that people are linked together in their efforts.
- Make certain that people who need extra support get it.

- Reassure people that they will have access to what they need to succeed.
- Set a pace to allow everyone to "keep up."
- Provide people with a comprehensive view of the destination and the obstacles and challenges.
- Clarify the process for moving forward and ensuring everyone's success.
- Personally sacrifice for the "common" good in times of extreme crisis.
- Make certain the workload is balanced for everyone.
- Make certain you have sufficiently budgeted to allow new ideas to be fully and thoroughly implemented.
- Consistently communicate key messages to all areas and levels of the organization.
- Empower people to take action.
- Reorganize your teams for more effective performance.
- Give people sufficient time to try their ideas.

SECONDARY ROLE EMPHASIS

Organizations must be taken in a new direction for a variety of reasons. Because situations differ, so must the roles you play as a leader. Although important to achieve success over the long term, certain roles may need to receive only secondary emphasis in the short term. These roles are:

- Nurturing leader
- Developmental leader

Nurturing Leader: Solidifying Why I Should Follow You

The role of the nurturing leader can be used to strike the appropriate balance between heading in the new direction with the people who are willing and able to go versus choosing an easier-to-achieve destination or bringing everyone along at a slower pace. If you have plenty of time to achieve your new direction or if the people in your organization in general are particularly nervous or uncertain they can succeed in the new direction, consider the following actions as you focus on the role of the nurturing leader:

- Regularly check how everyone is doing emotionally, psychologically, and physically.
- Strive to understand and reduce the limitations of others.

- Show individuals the progress they are making.
- Be honest about people's abilities when you focus on developing people.

Developmental Leader: Solidifying How You Will Help Me Get There

The developmental leader can capitalize on the nature of a major change effort to develop people. You can develop people's strategic thinking or global perspective by allowing them to help you define the new direction. You can develop people's analytical thinking and attention to detail by allowing them to participate in defining the path for the new direction, the "how" your organization will achieve this new destination.

Most change efforts require new skills. Therefore it makes good business sense to provide training (at a minimum, training is typically less expensive than firing existing personnel and hiring new people). If you have adequate time to achieve your new direction, if you have individuals who clearly understand the new direction and who want to follow you, and if risks of developing them are minimal, consider the following actions:

- Find out what people have to contribute.
- Allow people to contribute the expertise they have collected from other experiences.
- Give people the chance to examine their challenges from a different perspective.
- Challenge the group so they think in more creative and innovative ways.
- Understand the capabilities of your group.

ADDITIONAL ROLES

Certain actions within the roles of trusting leader, custodial leader, and inspiring leader may also help you successfully achieve your new direction within this context. While focusing on the primary and secondary roles, capitalize on opportunities to display the actions described next.

Trusting Leader

- Celebrate the achievement of others.
- Give authority to people to whom you have given responsibility.
- Do not punish the bearer of bad news.
- Act on others' ideas when appropriate.

- Recognize that people's fears are their realities.

Custodial Leader

- Ensure creative and innovative ideas are celebrated, not simply tolerated.
- Identify the organization's heroes and ensure that their stories are known by all.
- Protect what has transcended past generations and must transcend future generations.

Inspiring Leader

- Remind people their destination is better than where they currently are.
- Remind people that, by working together, any obstacles will be easily overcome.
- Exhibit the confidence and drive needed to inspire others.

WHEN IT'S TIME TO CHANGE THE LEADERSHIP ROLE EMPHASIS

There are two triggers that require you to consider shifting your emphasis on the four primary leadership roles. First, if resistance greatly diminishes, review Chapter 5 for advice on which leadership roles to emphasize when leading an organization in a new direction when people are open to change.

The second trigger occurs when you begin making significant progress toward your goals. This becomes obvious when you start achieving your short-term goals (remember those metrics you set up when flexing your working leader role) and people better understand what they need to do. If resistance continues, you will need to maintain a focus on the roles of trusted leader and strategic leader. This will help you gain people's trust and increase their understanding of why they need to change, thus allowing them to follow you in the new direction. You also need to continue to focus on the role of supportive leader to ensure that people are getting the support they need to be successful.

Given enough progress, you can move away from the role of the working leader, instead emphasizing the role of the custodial leader. Focus on the custodial leader role to stress how this change in direction is part of the natural evolution of your organization and how it connects to the organization's successful past and transitions everyone toward a successful future. This helps lock in the changes you are making to the status quo way the organization performs its tasks.

If you have a larger scope of responsibilities, you may find that some areas are making progress while others are not; some areas are showing resistance while others are not. If this is the case, you will need to treat each area according to its particular context.

IN PRACTICE[1]

The Scenario

Derek Carissimi may be one of the nation's leading human resources (HR) professionals. During the last 15 years, he has held leadership positions in several health care systems and medical centers. Carissimi is a change agent. He typically enters previously successful HR organizations currently considered to be in need of improvement or enhancement. Although the HR organization within which Carissimi leads is not at risk of closing, senior management brings him on board specifically to take the HR organization in a new direction.

In one case, the medical center in which Carissimi entered not only had previously been successful, it was recognized in the health care industry as being a leading emergent care facility and had a reputation of being where "I want to be taken if involved in a serious accident or otherwise in need of specialized emergency care." Although the health system had garnered such a good reputation, it was faltering in the eyes of many and the phrase had come to include the following modifier, "but when I wake up, I will want you to get me out of there and into one of the other local medical centers."

Such a paradox in health care proves interesting: a health system's emergent care—by many standards—can be exemplary, but subsequent patient care can be considered marginal. Senior management considered this situation to be fueled in part by the health system's HR organization. Tasked with helping recruit, assimilate (through a new employee orientation), and retain (through a variety of organization development programs and initiatives) quality health care workers, the HR organization had slipped in recent years. It was considered by many both inside and outside the health system to be in need of improvement.

Prior success created an environment in which many within the HR community did not recognize the need for improvement. A variety of external organizations, such as the Joint Commission on Accreditation of Healthcare Organizations (JCAHO), had previously recognized the health care system's effectiveness, and nursing administrators still complimented recruiters for the caliber of nurses being recruited into the health system. Unfortunately, senior management was concerned with what the next JCAHO assessment might reveal, and fewer recruiters were receiving fewer compliments.

Carissimi joined the health care system as Senior Vice President of Human Resources, with the mandate of enhancing the HR organization and improving the value it brought to the health system.

Leadership Actions: Why Should I Follow You?

Carissimi is action-oriented and goal-driven. He joined the health care system with two goals in mind: (1) to take the HR organization from its current to a much higher level of effectiveness, and (2) to help the health care system's HR professionals move from their current levels to much higher levels of success. Carissimi did not "hit the ground running" when he initially entered the organization, for he realized he had to:

- Further understand the culture and practices of the organization, so that he could leverage the positives and address the challenges in a planned and purposeful manner
- Gain people's confidence in his motives, vision, and personal style, so that they would willingly accompany him in the direction the organization would now be headed
- Reduce people's fears of changes likely to be made in the organization and how those changes might impact them and their careers, so that they could focus on the new direction and on what they must personally do to contribute to the organization's short- and long-term success

First, Carissimi met with his key internal stakeholders, including the health care system's board of directors and vice presidents of key stakeholder groups, such as nursing. He used these meetings to determine their perceptions about the HR organization, to identify areas of potential improvement, and to obtain their views on what would need to occur for them to consider HR an effective and efficient organization. Second, through one-on-one conversations and small group meetings, he attempted to learn as much as he could about the HR organization and its people. He strove to find out what motivated them, why they worked at that particular health care system, what they did that gave them a sense of accomplishment, and what they did that gave them a deep sense of satisfaction. He also explored how their satisfaction was impacted by what happened to them or to the co-workers, patients, and patients' families around them.

These meetings provided the information and data Carissimi needed for his subsequent decisions and actions, and cued him to actions, behaviors, and accomplishments worthy of reward and recognition. Throughout these meetings, Carissimi not only solicited needed information, but he in turn shared key sound bites with those in attendance. He introduced and reinforced the core message that health care as an industry is quickly changing, and that HR organizations within health care must also change; otherwise they (at best) become outdated or (worse) a thing of the past. He also shared the following message with anyone who would listen: that the upcoming changes would not only allow HR to bring more value to the health care system, but they in turn would give the HR professionals a heightened sense of accomplishment, pride, and self-esteem. As Carissimi identified and began working with select HR team members to address various opportunities for improvement, he also identified, recognized, and applauded those things HR was currently doing that were right and consistent with the way:

- HR professionals were *now* expected to think, behave, and perform
- The HR organization would be expected to operate in the *future*

Although Carissimi recognized the need to introduce new values and a new vision to the organization, he sought out opportunities through departmental meetings, luncheons with the vice president, and HR forums to involve others in determining how the vision and values would become an organization reality. He actively worked to broaden his zone of influence by incorporating key messages into departmental communiqués and a weekly newsletter.

Throughout his initial weeks and months at the health care system, Carissimi kept the CEO and COO apprised of his plan and actions and tested to make sure they were willing to contribute to, support, and advocate his actions. In addition, he sought out opportunities to present to his colleagues on the leadership team. Whenever given a chance, he introduced and then reinforced the following messages:

- As everyone on the leadership team understood, the health care profession is being challenged to do more with less.
- Although perhaps not as obvious or intuitive, the HR organization is also being challenged to do more with less.
- As a result, just as with the health care profession, that which contributed to human resources' previous success is not what will drive its future success.
- By building the HR team and through HR team building, the HR organization will rise up to meet the challenges before it.

- By working together, our team of HR professionals will not only survive, but thrive.

Leadership Actions: Where Are You Leading Me?

When taking an organization in a new direction, Carissimi believes that it is important (1) for the right team to be in place (if not, take steps to build the team or get the right team in place) and (2) that the organization be a high-performing team by ensuring, for example, that:

- The personal styles of team members complement each other
- Frameworks are in place to facilitate the team's managing disagreement and conflict
- Processes are in place to facilitate problem solving and decision making

Carissimi places such strong emphasis on team and teamwork because he truly believes—given the challenges organizations face today—that success can be achieved only by individuals acting responsibly and teams of individuals working together to overcome the challenges before them. Consistent with this belief, Carissimi spent his initial weeks informally assessing the knowledge, skills, and abilities of his HR team. In addition to determining if they had the skills needed to help move the organization forward, he assured his HR team members that as long as they were committed to the values, mission, and vision of the organization, he would see that they received needed coaching, counseling, and/or training to firm up their skill set. Coupled with this assurance were the following:

- The plan for the HR organization's moving forward
- Key strategies and tactics for making that movement occur
- Metrics with which to measure progress and success

In those few instances where individuals did not wish to think and act in accordance with the "new" organization, Carissimi worked with them to find suitable job opportunities elsewhere within the health care system. When opportunities were not available internally, Carissimi worked with the individuals to identify job opportunities outside the organization. Carissimi received some pushback from certain managers within the health care system. To their concerns, he responded that treating these individuals right was not only important for them, but doing the right things for the right reasons sent an invaluable message to the survivors—that regardless of what transpires, we will treat you with the dignity and respect you deserve.

Leadership Actions: How Will You Help Me Get There?

Believing that role modeling is important ("not do as I say, but rather do as I do"), Carissimi rolled up his sleeves and helped his direct reports address challenges to which they had never been exposed. For example, when one of his directors assumed responsibility for the corporate child-care center and had not previously dealt with issues associated with state licensure requirements, Carissimi took the time to answer questions and provide the necessary guidance for the director to be successful. He also personally intervened when resistance surfaced outside the HR organization, such as when the communications department could not understand why HR needed to upgrade its telephone system to provide a higher level of service to its customers.

Carissimi asked his department of training and organization development to identify individual and organization-wide developmental needs and address those needs through a variety of coaching, counseling, and training solutions. In addition, he firmed up the performance management system (many in the HR organization had not recently been evaluated, nor had they received feedback on their performance) by setting new expectations and directing managers and supervisors to monitor and provide feedback on their subordinates' performance. Carissimi also aggressively sought out opportunities for HR professionals to perform and succeed. Some were asked to take responsibility for new projects; others were placed into different positions or assigned new or expanded responsibilities. As individuals tested new behaviors and saw that they could be successful, and as their successes were recognized, Carissimi discovered that much of the fear that had surfaced on his arrival disappeared. As individuals tested new behaviors and saw that they would be supported even if they did not meet with 100 percent success, Carissimi found that much of the anxiety associated with the new ways of doing things subsided. As personal triumphs and team successes were celebrated, Carissimi found the subtle message to be exceptionally powerful: "this is what you are capable of accomplishing and this is the level of success to which you can personally aspire and achieve."

After taking several HR organizations into new directions, Carissimi now stresses the importance of the leader functioning in this context:

- Taking the time to understand what he or she is hoping to accomplish in terms of self, the organization, and the professionals within the organization
- Communicating and reinforcing messages about (1) the need for the change in direction, and (2) how by assuming personal responsibility

and by functioning as a team the organization will not only survive the challenges it faces, it will thrive
- Emphasizing the fact that, although the organization is headed in a new direction, each and every person retains control over his or her career
- Focusing on team capabilities, professionalism, and team member loyalty to the profession and its underlying code of ethics
- Introducing and reinforcing—in different ways, at different times— the new vision as well as the plan (including strategies and tactics) for attaining that vision

DISCUSSION QUESTIONS

1. What actions did Carissimi display that typified the roles of trusted leader, strategic leader, working leader, and supportive leader?
2. How were these roles integrated?
3. Which of the actions are most valuable to a leader being asked to move individuals from a successful state in a new direction when there is resistance to change?

SEVEN

Using Your Light to Redirect: The Plight of the Knight in Shining Armor

Many of us have likely daydreamed of being a knight in shining armor riding in at the last moment to save someone. In fact, we are confident that in a variety of ways some of you have been a knight in shining armor to someone else. The situations can include anything from life-and-death situations to opening the door for someone with arms full of packages.

Perhaps you have dreamed about being swept up on the knight's horse and riding off to a life of happily-ever-after. In such situations, few of us focus on the circumstances from which we may need to be rescued, choosing instead to direct our attention to the happily-ever-after future state.

Literature is full of references to the knight in shining armor who comes in to slay the dragon, fight off the evil knight, drive out the trolls, or destroy the invading army. In fact, a search on the word "knight" on a popular Internet bookstore produced a list of 8,201 books.

Some of these rescue tales have odd twists. One of our favorites is a children's book by Robert Munsch, *The Paper Bag Princess*.[1] In this story, young Princess Elizabeth was planning to one day marry Prince Ronald. Unfortunately a dragon strikes, destroys the castle, and carries off the prince. The young princess, with all her clothes burned up, dons a paper bag and heads off to the dragon's lair to rescue her prince. After tricking the dragon (you have to read the book to find out how), she heads into the dragon's cave to rescue the prince. Prince Ronald takes one look at her face smudged with ashes and her paper bag outfit and demands that she leave and return to save him when she looks more like a real princess. Princess Elizabeth responds that Ronald may look like a real prince, but he is a bum. She then dances off into the sunset—alone.

The organization version of the knight in shining armor is the turnaround. In a turnaround situation the organization is on the verge of failure or has failed. This could include bankruptcy, excessive turnover, insufficient membership levels, poor internal or external customer service, loss of confidence in a departmental function, or any set of circumstances that threaten an organization's existence.

Why do we call it the *plight* of the knight in shining armor? After all, saving people is what knights are trained to do. The answer is twofold. First, saving people is not always simple and easy. Second, like the prince in *The Paper Bag Princess*, not everyone will want you to save them.

If the story of Princess Elizabeth seems a bit far-fetched, consider the plight of the lifeguard. Those trained to save swimmers from drowning are taught how to physically disable people who, in their panic, threaten to drown themselves (along with the lifeguard). It is natural that when threatened, people panic and attempt to fight off the very person trying to save them.

If you are expected to be the knight in shining armor, the person selected to come in and save the organization by taking it to a new future of happily-ever-after, this is the section is for you. If you are being asked to lead an organization in a new direction from a state of failure, this section will provide concrete advice on how you can be successful in your plight.

DESCRIPTION OF THE SITUATION

The context in this setting is that the leader needs to take the organization in a new direction from a state of failure. (Please note, sometimes the "new" direction an organization must take is, in fact, the "old" direction that they had simply wandered from.) This could involve a complete business turnaround or replacing a failed: strategy, technology, business process, or initiative. It can also involve "fixing" a department that is failing to successfully perform the function for which it was designed or "righting" a nonprofit, not-for-profit, governmental, or municipal organization that is no longer achieving its desired goals.

INITIAL FOCUS OF THE LEADER

When trying to take people in a new direction from a failed or failing state, you should already have the new direction in mind before accepting the role, or you should be able to quickly establish a new direction after a brief diagnostic period. It is then critical that you use your leadership to redirect members of the organization. Initially, you must redirect them to focus on the new direction and what is causing the current direction to fail. You will also have to redirect their *energy* toward moving in the new direction. This means there may be many things they have gotten used to doing in a certain way that will now have to be performed in a different manner.

Some will view your efforts as the efforts of a knight in shining armor riding in to save: jobs, the company, the organization, or the goals to which they once aspired. Yet, there will be those who cooperate and those who, despite their desire to be saved, panic (causing the organization's performance to *further* deteriorate).

Others will view you as Prince Ronald viewed Princess Elizabeth. We don't recommend that you turn around and dance off into the sunset when faced with this resistance. We do suggest that you identify those who, no matter what you do, will not want to go in the new direction and not waste time trying to convince them. Rather work around them or take steps to replace them.

We have to share one caveat for this context. The advice contained in this section is specific to leadership actions. Turnarounds can be complex situations. We are *not* attempting to give the technical advice to deal with failures in finance, operations, human resources, products, services, or anything else that may have contributed to a failed state. We *are* attempting to provide you with the advice necessary for you to use your leadership skills to enable your technical expertise to be successful.

PRIMARY ROLE EMPHASIS

To establish your direction and gain a critical mass of followers, four roles are of primary importance:

- Trusted leader
- Strategic leader
- Supportive leader
- Working leader

If you are being asked to lead an organization from a failing or failed state, you are likely either new to the organization or new to your role in the organization. Employees in a failed or failing organization desire to have the organization continue to be viable, but they typically distrust anyone's attempt to change the organization or them, especially if you are new to the organization. In this context, you must first establish your role of trusted leader to gain people's confidence so they are willing to make the needed changes in their mindsets and behaviors.

Once this "enabling" role of trusted leader is adequately established, you have access to the support you need to be successful in additional roles. Emphasizing the role of strategic leader gives you the viewpoint you need to continue to stress and communicate your path forward. Emphasizing the role of working leader helps you establish with clarity the operational aspects of the strategy. Flexing the supportive leader role helps your followers accomplish their goals. How to apply these roles, and suggested actions, are described next.

Why Should I Follow You? Trusted Leader

Trusted leader is one of the three enabling roles that lay the foundation for you to be successful in all of the other roles. Members of a poorly performing organization are reluctant to trust leaders. After all, in their minds it was likely a leader that got them in this situation. Because the organization's current actions are taking it down the path (or has already led it) to failure, you cannot trust others to know what to do to change course or how to correct the situation. Therefore, the role of trusting leader should not be emphasized.

Also, in a failure situation you have hard realities that must be addressed. Chances are that some people will lose jobs or will have to give up traditional ways of performing that perhaps are near and dear to them. Thus an initial emphasis on the role of nurturing leader may have the negative impact of causing people to believe that things are going to be "all right." This can result in a situation where it will be hard to overcome inertia and move people down the new path.

When you strive to build the confidence in others to follow your leadership, you will find that you have a mixture of people who want and are ready to be rescued along with people who want to be rescued but, because of panic driven by the situation, resist you. Honesty and consistency of actions and words will go a long way toward winning the confidence of these people. Do not use fear as a motivation technique, as it will tend to increase panic, causing some to lose focus on the new direction and possibly dragging others down with them as in the example of the drowning swimmer.

It will be wise to remember that you will also have several "Prince Ronalds" in the organization—those who do not want to be "rescued" by you. There is nothing you can do to change their attitude. You will either need to work around them or you will need to remove them from their position and replace them with someone likely to embrace the needed changes.

Consider the appropriateness of the following actions that contribute to establishing the role of the trusted leader:

- Tell the truth, the whole truth, and nothing but the truth.
- Lead by example.
- Admit your mistakes.
- Collaborate with others.
- Keep your promises.
- Do not expend needless energy blaming others.
- Spend time building people up instead of tearing them down.
- Do not motivate by fear.
- Consider the needs of others first.
- Consistently be open and honest, even when it "hurts."
- Ask those closest to you to take the same risks you are asking of others.
- Advocate for your people.
- Share your fears.
- Assess your intentions.
- Accurately communicate the opinions of others even when you disagree.
- Be consistent in your actions.

Where Are You Leading Me? Strategic Leader

Along with working to gain people's trust, you must communicate the new direction. As mentioned earlier, it is important that you walk into a failed situation already knowing the direction you want to take the organization or being willing to determine that direction after a short diagnostic period. Therefore you need to devote most of your efforts to redirecting people's attention toward the new direction and making certain they understand the need to change from their current path. To achieve this, consider the following actions of the strategic leader:

- Share what you see with others.
- Focus everyone's attention on where you are going.
- Stress the urgent need for people to move forward.
- Try to see things from a different perspective.
- Help others focus on the overall mission rather than on the day-to-day challenges and crises.
- Reinvent your industry instead of trying simply to lead it.

This last bullet deserves a quick explanation. It comes into play most often when an entire industry is failing. In this situation, there can be a tremendous prize for the first organization to develop a new model, technology, or process for achieving the goals of the organization.

How Will You Help Me Get There? Working Leader and Supportive Leader

Once people start trusting you and begin understanding the direction you have communicated, you must help them begin moving in the new direction. You accomplish this by emphasizing the roles of the working leader and the supportive leader. Because of the nature of the turnaround, the progression to these roles must happen extremely rapidly.

When it comes to heading in a new direction, people frequently do not know how to begin. Use the role of the working leader to redirect people to a new way of accomplishing both their work and the work of the organization. Explain how they need to work differently and give them the feedback they must have to know if they are accomplishing things in the appropriate manner and if their efforts are achieving the desired results. Consider the following actions as you emphasize the role of the working leader:

- Help align everyone to the common goal.
- Focus on the details.
- Work among—and with—others to solve problems.
- Manufacture quick victories.
- Make certain you adequately supply people with the tools they need.
- At the end of the day, review today's actions and plan for tomorrow.
- Monitor, measure, and communicate progress.
- Balance "hard" and "soft" measures.
- Remain mentally agile and apply personal creativity to the situation at hand.

Redirecting an organization from a failing path to a successful one is challenging work for everyone. It is imperative that you do everything possible to give people the support they need to be successful. Individual successes will combine into larger successes, which will serve to alter the direction of the organization toward the "happily-ever-after" state, which we all hope the knight in shining armor will take us. As you emphasize the role of the supportive leader, consider the following actions:

- Make certain that people are linked together in their efforts.
- Make certain that people who need extra support get it.
- Reassure people that they will have access to what they need to succeed.
- Provide people with a comprehensive view of the destination and the obstacles and challenges.

- Clarify the process for moving forward and ensuring everyone's success.
- Personally sacrifice for the "common" good in times of extreme crisis.
- Consistently communicate key messages to all areas and levels of the organization.
- Reorganize your teams for more effective performance.

SECONDARY ROLE EMPHASIS

No organizational turnaround is exactly the same. Variations to the turnaround scenario may require different nuances in the emphasis of the leadership roles. In some situations a secondary emphasis on the roles of custodial leader and nurturing leader may prove useful.

Custodial Leader: Solidifying Where You Are Leading Me

There are two situations when a secondary emphasis on the role of the custodial leader may be helpful:

- The organization you are attempting to redirect is part of a larger organization that has a very strong identity, and the organization you are leading must fit within that identity.
- You are in danger of altering the organization so much that your customers or constituents may no longer recognize it as the same organization.

If either of these situations fits, you should consider the following actions:

- Protect what has transcended past generations and must transcend future generations.
- Focus on what has fueled past success.
- Identify the organization's heroes and ensure that their stories are known by all.
- Ensure creative and innovative ideas are celebrated, not simply tolerated.

Nurturing Leader: Solidifying How You Will Help Me Get There

Secondary emphasis on the role of nurturing leader may also provide some value. As previously mentioned, however, this role can also have a negative effect. If you find that people are becoming incapable of forward progress because of fear and stress, consider the following actions:

- Regularly check how everyone is doing emotionally, psychologically, and physically.
- Focus your attention on calming the fears of people.
- Show individuals the progress they are making.
- Strive to understand and reduce the limitations of others.
- Be honest about people's abilities when you focus on developing people.

ADDITIONAL ROLES

Certain actions within the roles of trusting leader, developmental leader, and inspiring leader may also help you successfully achieve your new direction. While focusing on the primary and secondary roles, capitalize on opportunities to display the actions described next.

Trusting Leader

- Celebrate the achievement of others.
- Give authority to people to whom you have given responsibility.
- Do not punish the bearer of bad news.
- Act on others' ideas when appropriate.
- Recognize that people's fears are their realities.

Developmental Leader

- Find out what people have to contribute.
- Allow people to contribute the expertise they have collected from other experiences.
- Give people the chance to examine their challenges from a different perspective.
- Challenge the group so that they think in more creative and innovative ways.
- Understand the capabilities of your group.

Inspiring Leader

- Remind people their destination is better than where they currently are.
- Remind people that, by working together, any obstacles will be easily overcome.
- Exhibit the confidence and drive needed to inspire others.

WHEN IT'S TIME TO CHANGE THE LEADERSHIP ROLE EMPHASIS

At some point in the turnaround process, it will become obvious that you are making progress. You will see that a significant portion of people are clear on the direction you are headed, understand what they need to do within their roles to achieve this direction, and are starting to accomplish some of the goals you have identified for them.

At this point, continue to gain momentum for what you are trying to do by shifting emphasis away from the four primary leadership roles. If you have been successful in the strategic leader role, the new direction should be clearly understood by everyone. If they are making progress and support structures are in place, you should be able to decrease your emphasis on the working leader and supportive leader roles.

You should continue to emphasize the trusted leader role. The organization may be making progress in the turnaround, but that progress can be fragile. You must take steps to maintain people's trust, in case you still have hard decisions to make. However, since people are not only understanding the new strategic direction but generating some early successes, you have the opportunity to use their abilities. This can include emphasizing the role of trusting leader by giving people greater responsibility in contributing to the success of the new direction. It can also include a focus on the developmental leader role and using the turnaround situation to provide some unique developmental opportunities. Highlight the nurturing leader role to begin to deal with the emotional and psychological impacts of the turnaround. Finally, if people are getting worn out during the time it takes to turn around the organization, you may need to leverage the inspiring leader role to remind them of why they need to work so hard and of the benefits that success will reap.

WHEN SPEED IS OF THE ESSENCE

There are times when the current organization has failed so dismally that it is in imminent danger of ceasing to exist. This is most apparent from a financial perspective. You may no longer have the cash to purchase raw materials or pay bills. You may not have the cash to meet payroll. Your bond ratings may have been lowered to junk status. When this is the case, speed is of the essence.

Here you must greatly focus your leadership actions to succeed. If you are in such a situation, consider adjusting the actions previously listed as follows:

Primary Role Emphasis

Trusted Leader

- Actively orchestrate opportunities to "do the right thing for the right reason."

Strategic Leader

- Don't worry about trying to reinvent your industry.

Supportive Leader

- Focus on quickly providing support where it is most needed and will be most evident to customers and to individuals within the organization.

Working Leader

- Establish short-term objectives and work with others to achieve them.
- Incorporate measurement and communication into all aspects of your day.
- Make certain that people in crucial areas have the tools they need to succeed.
- Constantly apply actions and results against the short-term objectives.
- Help followers focus on those details having the most impact on pressure points.
- Manufacture victories likely to resonate with followers and key stakeholders.
- Remain healthy and mentally agile.

Secondary Role Emphasis

Custodial Leader

- Ensure creative and innovative ideas are adopted, acted on, and, to the extent possible, duplicated.
- Stress that the only way for the effort, work, and success of past generations to survive is to work together now to ensure that the organization survives.

Nurturing Leader

- Don't worry about regularly checking how everyone is doing emotionally and psychologically—you don't have the time.

Additional Role

Developmental Leader

- As quickly as possible, find out what people have to contribute.
- Emphasize the importance of people contributing expertise from other experiences.

IN PRACTICE

The Scenario

William Roosevelt (not real name) joined Perktor Industries (not real name) in 1984. Over the years he had been promoted through a variety of positions with ever increasing responsibilities. In the mid-1990s, Perktor enrolled Roosevelt in an internal leadership development program designed to prepare Perktor's next generation of general managers. Roosevelt excelled in this program and greatly impressed the company.

Three years later, Roosevelt was given an opportunity to serve in a general manager (GM) role. Perktor had a division that was languishing. A stellar performer several years earlier, the division had lost its focus on the key elements of the business model that drove profitability. Employee morale was low. Several good employees had resigned, sure that they were leaving the ship before it sank. Of the employees who were still there, many had given up hope but were riding it out because of feelings of loyalty. Others were still there because they did not understand how bad things really were. Roosevelt's charge was to turn the division around or it would be shuttered or sold.

Leadership Actions: Why Should I Follow You?

When Roosevelt started in the GM role, the division had not been profitable for "eighteen quarters" as the CEO of the parent company was fond of emphasizing. Before he accepted this new position, it was already clear to Roosevelt that he needed to change the current path the business was taking. His goal was to get the division back on track with the elements that had initially made it successful—a focus on growth and profitability through easy-to-use products. It was also clear to Roosevelt that, in the current competitive environment, the necessary growth could be achieved through international growth. To achieve this goal, Roosevelt's initial focus was to instill confidence in employees that the business was viable for the long term, the company was interested in fixing the division, and Roosevelt was the person capable of leading them to this success.

The previous GM had implemented a paper-driven approval process that required his signature for all major capital decisions. While necessary, this had greatly slowed down the decision process (the previous GM did not respond to written requests for approval in a timely manner). People had to wait weeks, and in some cases months, before their requests were addressed. Roosevelt decided to get people to trust him, and to convince them that the parent company was serious about improving the division, by fixing this lack of responsiveness and doing it in a way that caught people's attention. He announced to all that he would respond to any request for his approval within three days. His secretary then started time stamping when he received the request and time stamping when he returned it to the requestor. Word quickly spread through the division. "Roosevelt got back to me in four hours." "Roosevelt approved my request in one hour." "Roosevelt got back to me in ten minutes!" Roosevelt was quickly becoming viewed as being a man of his word.

Roosevelt did other things to prove that his words and actions were consistent. The office culture was one of show up a bit late and leave a bit early. Roosevelt asked his direct reports to get in a little bit earlier and stay until the work was done. However, it was hard to beat Roosevelt into the office and he was usually the one turning out the lights at night.

Roosevelt insisted that his department heads keep their costs low. Although the previous GM had emphasized the same message for the most recent six quarters, he was not willing to give up the company's sky box, using it as a personal perk. With a few weeks left in the season, Roosevelt held an office raffle announcing that the winners would get to attend the "last" games in the skybox. The combination of offering the tickets to others along with making it obvious that he would not be renewing the skybox proved an effective way for Roosevelt to demonstrate that he didn't exclude himself from needing to cut costs.

Leadership Actions: Where Are You Leading Me?

While working to get people to trust him, Roosevelt concurrently worked to redirect people's focus to the elements that would make them successful: international growth, easy-to-use products, and high profit margin. To achieve this goal, he had to address two issues: poor communication and a lack of effective business metrics. He was both direct and consistent in communicating throughout the division the current state, where they needed to head, and how they were going to get there. He instituted quarterly calls to unit heads to reinforce these messages and discuss what was working and what was not working. Every three months he sent out a division-wide "State of the Business" e-mail reinforcing the strategy, describing progress, and providing news about what was happening in the business. Throughout these communications he was honest about the issues they still faced. He also let people know that the issues they were facing could not be fixed overnight, but he helped them to see that the division was making progress. His question to his employees became, "Are we better off than we were last month?"

Roosevelt also discovered the absence of effective business metrics. Employees could see how their unit was performing in any one month, but it was difficult to determine how effectively individual units were executing the year-to-date business plan. Roosevelt established a measurement system that made it easy to see how each unit was performing against the plan for the year. At the time Roosevelt considered this change something minor, but in retrospect he believes this had a huge impact in helping him reinforce his messages of:

- Speaking honestly about the current business state
- Clearly describing where the business needs to head
- Articulating the steps everyone needs to take

Leadership Actions: How Will You Help Me Get There?

To help his division successfully execute the strategy, Roosevelt continued to communicate, communicate, communicate. He visited the operating units and recognized people for their efforts. He always followed up his visits with personal notes describing what he saw and what he appreciated. He strengthened his leadership team, working hard to replace those who left with quality performers. He began a series of casual interactions between front office and manufacturing personnel to help everyone understand that their efforts toward improving business performance were linked to the efforts of others.

As the division moved forward in its journey to turn around the business, people were required to do things differently than in the past. Roosevelt was patient in the help he provided. He first described to people what they needed to do. If their performance on the task was not up to appropriate standards, Roosevelt spent additional time with the person clarifying his expectations, describing exactly what the end product should look like, setting up a time frame for when the work should get done, and creating check points along the way to make certain the effort stayed on track and on target.

Being a small division within a larger company had its own challenges. Certain reporting procedures required by the parent company were not clearly understood by people. Roosevelt coached them in how to provide the appropriate level of detail in the reports. He looked for opportunities for them to present to corporate staff. In some instances he allowed people to fail in little ways so that they would better understand the expectations of the corporate staff.

After 18 consecutive quarters of losses, Perktor was profitable last year and is currently ahead of plan for this year. The flow of exiting personnel has been stemmed and morale has increased. This year the division will be paying out employee bonuses for the first time in more than four years.

Roosevelt offers the following advice to people trying to lead in similar contexts:

- Make people aware of the current state of the business as soon as you can accurately describe it.
- Be direct when describing the current state of the business.
- Clearly define your vision and mission for the organization.
- Plainly articulate what you as a leader are going to do and how you are going to do it.
- Plainly articulate the strategic steps the organization will take.
- Give people the opportunity to opt out or sign on to the new direction.
- Move out the people who just sit.
- Establish and communicate metrics so that everyone can see the progress being made.
- Let people know that the business will not be turned around overnight.
- Keep asking, "Are we better off than we were last month?"

DISCUSSION QUESTIONS

1. What actions did Roosevelt display that typified the roles of trusted leader, strategic leader, working leader, and supportive leader?
2. How were these roles integrated?
3. Which of the actions are most valuable to a leader being asked to take an organization in a new direction from a failed state?

EIGHT

Using Your Light to Maintain: John Henry Knew What to Do

In childhood we grew up listening to stories of John Henry, learned mainly through poems and songs. There was an actual man by the name of John Henry, and there is much legend surrounding him.

John Henry *the man* was born in the 1840s or 1850s in North Carolina or Virginia. He worked for C&O Railroad as a steel-driver, using steel drills or spikes to drive holes into tunnel walls. Like all steel-drivers, John Henry had a partner, who would rotate the spike or drill after each blow of John Henry's hammer. John Henry worked on the work crew assigned to cut tunnels through treacherous terrain such as Oak Mountain, Alabama, and Big Bend Mountain, Ohio. Such mountains were frequently more than a mile thick. These projects typically required more than 1,000 employees and took several years to complete. Conditions inside the tunnels were challenging: the air was hot and stagnant, the tunnel frequently was full of thick smoke and dust, and the risk of cave-ins and landslides was constant. Historians agree that, in spite of such conditions, John Henry called on his personal drive and relied on his physical strength to consistently drill 10 to 20 feet into tunnel walls during his standard 12-hour shift. Hundreds of men perished while helping construct railroad tunnels; John Henry was one of them.

John Henry *the legend* was in his mid-40s, stood six feet tall, and weighed 200 pounds (this was huge for his day, the mid- and late-1870s). He was the fastest, strongest, and most powerful steel-driver who has ever worked for C&O or any other railroad. Using a 14-pound hammer, he drilled 20 or more feet into the tunnel wall each workday. He had a ravenous appetite, was a spirited man, and was an accomplished banjo player. Above all else, he took great pride in being a steel-driver.

The story goes that one day a salesman entered the C&O Railroad camp and boasted that his steam-powered drilling machine could out-drill *any* man. Taking strong exception to this claim, John Henry challenged the salesman to an all-day duel. Some stories suggest the contest occurred in the early 1870s; others suggest it occurred on September 20, 1887. Some stories suggest the contest occurred at Big Bend Mountain; others suggest it occurred at Oak Mountain. They all agree that at the end of the contest John Henry collapsed from exhaustion then regained consciousness just long enough to speak to his wife and to learn that he had won the race. Some stories say that John Henry drilled 27 1/2 feet that day, and the steam-powered machine drilled only 21 feet; others say that John Henry drilled 14 feet and the machine drilled only 9.

There are two lessons to be learned from the legend of John Henry. First, we are all given an opportunity to leave our mark on the world; we all have a chance to leave a lasting legacy. Success does not necessarily involve doing something extremely well one day and being recognized for that event the rest of your life or career; it more likely involves doing something consistently well every day, regardless of the circumstances or the environment within which you find yourself. We can all at times describe situations and conditions within which we work as being unfavorable. John Henry could have focused on the heat, the smoke, the dust, and the constant danger. However, through his tenacity to do the right thing day in and day out, and for standing up for his beliefs in the face of such adversity, John Henry became an inspiration for generations and an example of what a person can accomplish through perseverance.

Second, regardless of our position or the role we play, we all can impact our organization in a favorable way. Whether an executive, manager, foreman, or steel-driver, we can take immense pride in our effort, contribution, and accomplishment. Many agree that it takes courage and strength of conviction to carry an organization or a group of individuals through a crisis. The inspiration from the legend of John Henry comes not from his winning the one-day competition or dying as a result, but from his willingness and his eagerness to do a good job every day, the long-term impact of his steady and constant contribution, and the legacy he left behind.

If you are being asked to maintain the current path or state, this is the section for you. In other words, if you feel you need the strength and persistence of John Henry, read on!

DESCRIPTION OF THE SITUATION

The context we address in this section is perhaps the most common. It is a setting in which the leader is asked to maintain the current path or state of the organization. This context assumes the organization's vision, mission, and values are set and that they are being played out on a daily basis. This typically involves the leader maintaining the current strategy, technology, business processes, and initiatives. However, it also recognizes the need for organizations to continuously improve their performance and takes into account that the leader, while maintaining the current path or state, will undoubtedly refine the current strategy, upgrade technology, streamline, and otherwise enhance business processes and introduce new initiatives.

INITIAL FOCUS OF THE LEADER

If you are asked to maintain a current path or state of the organization, you must initially focus on:

- Maintaining or firming-up the credibility you have within the organization
- Taking steps to ensure that others within the organization follow your leadership

As you work to accomplish these goals, it will be important to remember what John Henry taught us. Being successful over the long run does not depend on the actions of a few, select "heroes." Rather, it depends on the effort and accomplishment of the "solid" majority. Although it seems to make intuitive sense to focus on heroes and their actions (and potentially spend an inordinate amount of time recognizing their deeds), it is also important to recognize the constant and consistent actions of the many. Again, John Henry's inspiration comes *not* from the daylong contest, but from the *many weeks, months, and years* that he, *and others like him,* drilled into the tunnel walls and the pride they all took in the quality and quantity of their work.

Your work environment is probably not marked by heat, smoke, dust, and constant danger; but there are undoubtedly elements that will impact the ability of you and your followers to focus, put forth your best effort, accomplish tasks as designed, and succeed in your goals. We meet few people these days who do not feel understaffed and overworked. Financial markets drive a short-term focus always asking, "What have you done for me lately?" Not-for-profits are finding people more reluctant to volunteer with the busyness of everyone's schedules. With these and other environmental factors at play, we recommend that you take steps to (1) give others confidence that you will *continue* supporting the current direction of the organization and (2) ensure that people continue respecting your role as their leader. Five leadership roles will help you do this.

PRIMARY ROLE EMPHASIS

If you need to use your leadership light to maintain the current direction, we recommend that you work to give others confidence in your continued support of the current direction and ensure that you maintain the respect of your followers. This can be accomplished by emphasizing the following five leadership roles:

- Custodial leader
- Trusting leader
- Nurturing leader
- Developmental leader
- Supportive leader

When asked to maintain a current path or state of the organization, your initial emphasis should be to maintain or enhance the role of custodial leader to demonstrate your continued and constant desire to lead the organization down its current path. In addition, focusing on the roles of trusting leader and nurturing leader will reinforce your credibility in the eyes of your followers. Once you have adequately reinforced these roles, we recommend that you use the role of supportive leader to help your followers accomplish their goals and developmental leader to make certain they have the required skill sets to be successful in the near term and, perhaps more important, the long term.

Why Should I Follow You? Custodial Leader

Maintaining the current path or state of the organization suggests maintaining over the long term. Above all else, the custodial leader strives to sustain momentum using actions that drive and support the organization's vision and key values for the long term and makes certain that the light of leadership never burns out. The custodial leader must do all that he or she can on a daily basis to ensure immediate and short-term success and, in doing so, must keep in the back of his or her mind that all leadership decisions and actions will influence and otherwise contribute to the organization's future success. In the end, the custodial leader must recognize that his or her decisions and actions will ultimately impact the organization that he or she leaves behind, including the organization's vision, strategies, technology, business processes, initiatives, and people.

If you are trying to get an organization to maintain its current path or its organizational state, your biggest enemy may be repetitiveness and the resulting boredom and lack of creativity. Within such a context, you must constantly and consistently point out what is truly important and how what each and every member of the organization does on a daily basis impacts the organization in a positive or negative (and very seldom, in a neutral) way. To heighten and/or reinforce your continued and constant desire to lead the organization down its current path, consider the appropriateness of the following actions of the custodial leader:

- Focus on what has fueled past success.
- Make certain that the light of leadership in your organization never burns out.
- Consider the long-term impact of your actions.
- Consider your impact on the environment.
- Ensure creative and innovative ideas are celebrated, not simply tolerated.
- Ensure that key challenges and triumphs are remembered.
- Identify the organization's heroes and ensure that their stories are known by all.
- Record the "whys" of decisions so that they can be archived for future reference.
- Ensure that today's strengths are applied to future challenges and opportunities.
- Protect what has transcended past generations and must transcend future generations.
- Strive to sustain the organization for the long term.

Where Are You Leading Me? Trusting and Nurturing Leader

Your demonstrating a continued and constant desire to lead the organization down its current path emphasizes to the followers that they should not expect marked changes in the intent, focus, or purpose of the organization. It also reinforces that they should continue doing what they currently do on a daily basis. Because the course has been set and the organization is on the right trajectory, the leader can now emphasize how members of the organization are to function to maximize effectiveness and optimize efficiencies. In such a situation, what will occur has already been established; you are on the right course and will gradually refine the strategy, upgrade technology, streamline and enhance business processes, and introduce new initiatives. Everyone in the organization should expect and strive to maintain the current course. Here you have an opportunity to emphasize how the members of the organization are to treat others while striving to accomplish the organization's mission and attain its vision, and in turn, how they can expect to be treated by others throughout the journey.

In many ways the success you have in maintaining the current direction depends on the consistency of not only your convictions, focus, words, and actions but on those of every member of your organization. Because there should already be great clarity around your current direction, you, as leader, have the opportunity to impact the consistency of others by turning over responsibility and authority to others—in essence trusting them to do their jobs without being told what to do. You can then serve in a capacity where you help others, as necessary, and course correct their focus, actions, and words to maintain the consistency necessary to be successful.

As you help others sustain a "John Henry" focus on the current path, consider the appropriateness of the following actions of the trusting leader:

- Allow others to lead.
- Give others permission to make mistakes.
- Reinforce good performance.
- Celebrate the achievement of others.
- Give authority to people to whom you have given responsibility.
- Act on others' ideas when appropriate.
- Seek ideas from others.
- Focus on the goal and let others worry about the how.
- When appropriate, act on the advice of others, even when you strongly disagree with them.
- Recognize that people's fears are their realities.
- Trust others enough to share your leadership responsibilities.

As you monitor and respond to the way your followers make the organization's mission and values real through their words and actions, consider the appropriateness of the following actions of the nurturing leader:

- Work to establish a sense of "family" within your organization.
- Regularly check how everyone is doing emotionally, psychologically, and physically.
- Learn from your direct reports, encouraging them to share their skills.
- Encourage people around you to more broadly share their skills.
- Focus your attention on the immediate needs of the people.

- Strive to understand and reduce the limitations of others.
- Spend time helping people get "little doses" of the challenges facing them.
- Ensure the voice of the minority is heard and taken into consideration.
- Focus more on people's development.
- Take steps to ensure that people are proud of how they are developing.
- Show individuals the progress they are making.
- Be honest about people's abilities when you focus on developing people.

How Will You Help Me Get There? Developmental Leader and Supportive Leader

Once people trust that there will be no marked changes in the intent, focus, or purpose of the organization and understand how they are to treat others as they maintain the current path, you then need to take steps to ensure that they have the knowledge, skills, and abilities to most fully contribute to the organization's vision and mission. This is accomplished by emphasizing the role of the developmental leader. The developmental leader ensures that no opportunities need be missed. This includes an individual not missing an opportunity because of a lack of personal development and the organization not missing an opportunity because of an absence of the necessary knowledge and skills. Consider the following actions as you emphasize the role of the developmental leader:

- Give people the chance to learn from others' expertise.
- In addition to celebrating success, share "lessons" with others so that they, too, may learn from your experiences.
- Give people a chance to discover how to accomplish their objectives.
- Find out what people have to contribute.
- Solicit input from others.
- Give others the opportunity to plot the path forward.
- Allow people to contribute the expertise they have collected from other experiences.
- Ask others their perception of what your role should be.
- Give people the chance to examine their challenges from a different perspective.
- Challenge the group so that they think in more creative and innovative ways.
- Give people an opportunity for broader experiences.
- Understand the capabilities of your group.

Successful organizations, even those maintaining the current path, rely on the achievements of their people to accomplish and produce optimal results. Otherwise, they do not deliver on the expectations set forth in their mission statement, nor are they likely to attain their vision. This is why it is crucial that the leader *support* those striving to maintain the current path. As you emphasize the role of the supportive leader, consider the following actions:

- Make certain that people are linked together in their efforts.
- Make certain that people who need extra support get it.
- Reassure people that they will have access to what they need to succeed.
- Set a pace to allow everyone to "keep up."
- Provide people with a comprehensive view of the destination and the obstacles and challenges.
- Clarify the process for moving forward and ensuring everyone's success.
- Personally sacrifice for the "common" good in times of extreme crisis.
- Make certain the workload is balanced for everyone.
- Make certain you have sufficiently budgeted to allow new ideas to be fully and thoroughly implemented.
- Consistently communicate key messages to all areas and levels of the organization.
- Empower people to take action.
- Reorganize your teams for more effective performance.
- Give people sufficient time to try their ideas.

SECONDARY ROLE EMPHASIS

Although important, certain roles may need to receive secondary emphasis when maintaining the current direction. These roles are:

- Trusted leader
- Working leader

Trusted Leader: Solidifying Why I Should Follow You

The role of the trusted leader can be used to strike the appropriate balance between an organization's maintaining the current path and its responding to unforeseen and unplanned forces. Operating in today's turbulent business environment, leaders recognize that the "space" within which the organization functions must be closely monitored, and the organization's strategic plan (and thus, the full gamut of its will and resources) must quickly change to respond to unforeseen and unplanned situations and circumstances. In today's environment, business as usual can quickly become business as unusual. Today's leader must therefore reinforce to his or her followers that if or when the organization's path needs to change, they can have the confidence that the leader will be there to lead them to the new destination. Seek out opportunities to instill the trust of your people by taking the following actions of the trusted leader:

- Tell the truth, the whole truth, and nothing but the truth.
- Lead by example.
- Admit your mistakes.
- Collaborate with others.
- Keep your promises.
- Spend time building people up instead of tearing them down.
- Consider the needs of others first.
- Consistently be open and honest, even when it "hurts."
- Ask those closest to you to take the same risks you are asking of others.
- Advocate for your people.
- Share your fears.
- Assess your intentions.
- Accurately communicate the opinions of others even when you disagree.
- Be consistent in your actions.

Working Leader: Solidifying How You Will Help Me Get There

When people trust that you will step up to unforeseen pressures, you need to actively engage them in addressing the challenges of the present. This is accomplished by emphasizing the role of the working leader. In maintaining the current direction, people should already understand where they are headed and how they are to get there. Use the role of the working leader to focus people on what their priorities should be and how their work needs to be done, and to reinforce how they are to think, behave, and act toward others while working toward achieving the desired results. Consider the following actions as you emphasize the role of the working leader:

- Help align everyone to the common goal.
- Focus on the details.
- Work among—and with—others to solve problems.

- Monitor, measure, and communicate progress.
- Manufacture quick victories.
- Make certain you adequately supply people with the tools they need.
- At the end of the day, review today's actions and plan for tomorrow.
- Be measurement driven.
- Remain mentally agile and apply personal creativity to the situation at hand.

ADDITIONAL ROLES

Certain actions within the roles of strategic leader and inspiring leader may also contribute to your success within this context. While focusing on the primary and secondary roles, capitalize on opportunities to exhibit the actions described next:

Strategic Leader

- Share what you see with others.
- Accept input from other sources.
- Show people the boundaries within which they operate.
- Focus everyone's attention on where you are going.
- Help others focus on the overall mission rather than on the day-to-day challenges and crises.
- Keep an eye on the competition.
- Try to see things from a different perspective.
- Learn more about your industry.

Inspiring Leader

- Show people how close they are to reaching their destination.
- Remind people that their destination is better than where they currently are.
- Reinforce that people are not alone in the challenges they face and that everyone will share together in the eventual rewards.
- Remind people of the dream that started them out on this journey.
- Remind people of what they have accomplished so far.
- Exhibit the confidence and drive needed to inspire others.
- Find out what your people do best and link it to the dream.
- Give people the opportunity to do what they do best, in pursuit of the dream.
- Articulate your dream, along with the dreams of the organization.
- Spend time encouraging others.

WHEN IT'S TIME TO CHANGE LEADERSHIP ROLE EMPHASIS

There are three triggers that require you to consider shifting your emphasis on the five primary leadership roles: (1) people begin to look around for additional challenges, or other factors combine to require you to set a new direction; (2) progress begins to bog down; and (3) the organizational context significantly changes.

If people begin to look around for additional challenges, or if other factors combine to require you to set a new direction, consider continuing to focus on the five primary roles while directing time and energy toward the role of strategic leader:

- Share what you see with others.
- Accept input from other sources.
- Show people the boundaries within which they operate.
- Focus everyone's attention on where you are going.
- Help others focus on the overall mission rather than on the day-to-day challenges and crises.
- Keep an eye on the competition.
- Try to see things from a different perspective.

If progress begins to bog down and if momentum waivers, consider moving away from the custodial leader, trusting leader, and developmental leader roles and place additional emphasis on the working leader and inspiring leader roles.

If the organization context significantly changes, consider moving away from the current leadership behaviors toward those that more closely match the new organizational context (described elsewhere in this section).

IN PRACTICE[1]

The Scenario

The North Carolina Justice Academy is considered by many to be one of the nation's leading law enforcement training academies. Created in 1973, it is a division of the North Carolina Department of Justice. The Justice Academy provides training programs for criminal justice personnel; provides technical assistance to criminal justice officials; and develops, publishes, and distributes criminal justice education and training materials. The Justice Academy provides services in areas such as management, supervision, criminal investigation, and traffic accident investigation. In addition, it conducts research and development and provides criminal justice courses at two campuses (one located in eastern North Carolina and one located in western North Carolina).

Dr. Martha A. Stanford has served as the director of the North Carolina Justice Academy for more than 20 years. Although Dr. Stanford entered an already successful organization, through her constant and consistent leadership she has made it more successful in terms of the breadth and quality of its services, the extent to which it meets the needs of its various stakeholders, and the manner in which it provides services to North Carolina's criminal justice community.

Serving directly at the discretion of the North Carolina Attorney General (and indirectly at the discretion of the North Carolina legislature and governor), it is noteworthy that Dr. Stanford has served several attorneys general, state legislatures, and governors. She has also received and continues to receive the support and advocacy of North Carolina Association of Chiefs of Police and North Carolina Sheriffs Association leadership.

The Justice Academy is composed of criminal justice professionals with a variety of educational credentials including law degrees and doctorates, an assortment of professional certifications and licensures, and a breadth of federal, state, and local criminal justice experiences. Coupled with this are the mindsets and perspectives of individuals tasked with embracing "every aspect of the criminal justice system by providing programs and working with other agencies to upgrade the system's practices and personnel."

Such mindsets and perspectives contribute to an environment in which a majority of the academy faculty and staff recognize the need for professionalism and continuous improvement. Evidence of this is the reputation that the Justice Academy has built over the past three decades and the extent to which (1) local, county, and state agencies within North Carolina send their criminal justice professionals to be trained by the Justice Academy and (2) training and development professionals from other states come to the Justice Academy to be trained, certified, and then to return to share lessons learned and best practices throughout their perspective state criminal justice training and development communities.

Dr. Stanford had previously served as an instructor-coordinator and a training manager with the Justice Academy, left to apply her knowledge and expertise elsewhere, and then returned to take the helm of the Justice Academy as its director. Upon her appointment as director, she was tasked by the North Carolina Attorney General to lead the Justice Academy into the 1990s and beyond in a way that capitalized on Justice Academy resources, built on the reputation that it had established, and took the criminal justice profession to higher levels of effectiveness and efficiency.

Leadership Actions: Why Should I Follow You?

When asked to assume leadership of the North Carolina Justice Academy, Dr. Stanford recognized the importance of initially demonstrating her desire to lead the organization down the path on which it was previously headed. While realizing that she would ultimately influence the manner in which the organization's mission and values played out, she understood that it was initially more important for the academy to maintain its momentum and not stumble in the eyes of:

• Key stakeholders who considered its services and products to be worthwhile and valuable
• Faculty and staff who had, over the previous 10 years, contributed to the academy's regional and national reputation

Dr. Stanford therefore initially shared a core message with the academy's key stakeholders (including police chiefs, sheriffs, legislatures, and other government officials) that the academy had built a solid reputation and would:

• Continue delivering services to build on its reputation
• Intensify its effort to find out what the North Carolina criminal justice needed from such an institution
• Further exceed the expectations placed on it through its interactions and offerings

Dr. Stanford met with each member of the Justice Academy, not only the faculty but also the staff responsible for supporting the faculty. During these meetings, she sent the following subtle messages to the faculty and staff:

• I am sincerely interested in making sure that we all recognize the important mission we have before us.
• I consider our working together as a team to be of paramount importance.
• As training and development professionals, we recognize the importance of lifelong learning and professional development.
• As the academy's new director, I will take steps to ensure that lifelong learning and professional development opportunities are available to the Justice Academy faculty and staff.

Dr. Stanford found the meetings with the internal and external stakeholders to be invaluable. From the external stakeholders, she gained insights about their perceptions and expectations, identified areas of organizational strength, and obtained their views on areas within the organization that could be improved on. When their recommendations were doable, she let them know she would do all she could to see that they were adopted. When their recommendations were faulty or lacked viability, she let them know she heard and understood what they said and shared her reasons why it was doubtful the suggestions could be adopted. From the internal stakeholders, Dr. Stanford learned about the inner workings of the Justice Academy (what you have to do to get things done around here) and its people including what accomplishments they were particularly proud of, what motivated them to choose a career in criminal justice, why they worked at the Justice Academy (versus some other federal, state, or local agency), and what gave them the deepest sense of meaningfulness and personal satisfaction.

The criminal justice community reported that the Justice Academy deserved its reputation and that, in general, law enforcement officials were pleased with services and products the Justice Academy provided. However, Dr. Stanford (as much as from what she did *not* hear as from what she *did* hear) recognized the need to firm up relationships with and expand/improve offerings to the sheriffs of North Carolina. In addition, she found the faculty and staff in need of new challenges and opportunities. While the North Carolina Justice Academy was doing a lot of things right, years of maintaining the current path had yielded static, rather than creative, ideas. Faculty and staff members voiced an interest in helping: update the organization's curriculum, enhance educational technology the academy employed, streamline its business processes, and offer new training and development opportunities to the criminal justice community. As faculty and staff left their "meeting with the director," they voiced excitement and optimism about the weeks and months to come.

During staff meetings and informal gatherings, Dr. Stanford talked about how in all the roles they play, faculty and staff impact the organization in a positive or negative way through their everyday actions. By thinking, acting, and treating each other as true professionals, they can upgrade the North Carolina criminal justice system's practices and personnel. During meetings and informal gatherings with her managers, she stressed the importance of their supporting the faculty and staff. At the Justice Academy, it was important for the management team to keep the right perspective. It was the frontline researcher, educator, trainer, supported by a team of staff members, who was bringing value to the criminal justice community. It was the responsibility of the management team to provide the support and resources the frontline needed to be successful. In short, Dr. Stanford stressed to the managers that they were responsible for creating and reinforcing an environment in which individuals could achieve and teams could flourish.

Leadership Actions: Where Are You Leading Me?

Dr. Stanford immediately recognized the importance of leading the Justice Academy down the path on which it was previously headed, for it was already providing services and products the criminal justice community considered to be worthwhile and valuable. Through personal analysis and conversations with key internal and external stakeholders, she attempted to identify factors that had contributed to the Justice Academy's previous success and that yielded the reputation it enjoyed throughout the state's (and to a slightly lesser degree, the nation's) criminal justice community. Her analysis revealed three critical success factors (which in all likelihood will not be a surprise to our readers): focus on quality, be service-driven, and strive to meet the needs and exceed the expectations of the customers. With her management team and key staff members, Dr. Stanford explored conditions within the Justice Academy that allowed it to focus on quality, be service-driven, and meet the needs and exceed the expectations of the customers.

She discovered that the Justice Academy had to continue hiring and retaining criminal justice training professionals who personally commit to:

- Providing quality training to students
- Putting the student's interest first
- Addressing student needs in a creative and innovative way
- Using the latest in instructional technology

She also discovered that she had to continue building the management team, so it would consist of individuals who personally commit to:

- Encouraging and supporting the faculty and staff's creative and innovative ideas
- Providing a work environment in which everyone is treated fairly and with dignity and respect
- Helping establish and maintain inviolable standards of quality and professionalism
- Identifying and addressing the faculty and staff's professional development needs

In terms of her own leadership behavior, Dr. Stanford learned:

- She does not have to have all of the answers. She points out that the Justice Academy hires only "the best of the best," so why should she not call on them for their insights, suggestions, and recommendations?
- The importance of recognizing that there are multiple paths to one's (or an organization's) achievement and success. She points out that

her ideas may not be the best, nor may her suggested or preferred path be the most effective or efficient. In considering options, she stresses the importance of (1) thinking through and being able to support one's rationale, (2) considering contingencies, and (3) selecting the path based on its individual merits.

- She does not operate within a vacuum. She points out that both the decision she makes and the manner in which she makes it, communicates it, and reinforces it, speaks volumes about what she truly values and what she, in turn, feels is important from an organizational perspective. Here, she emphasizes the importance of understanding yourself and what you hope to accomplish as a leader, including how you plan to influence the members of your organization.

In her one-on-one conversations, management and staff meetings, and when responding to incidents and situations, Dr. Stanford emphasized that she and all Justice Academy personnel should treat others, and expect to be treated by others, in a way that:

- Leaves them feeling like they are part of an extended family
- Shows that they will receive the support they need, not only when times are good, but when faced with challenge and adversity
- They know they will not be "punished" if they make a mistake when trying something new or attempting the near impossible

Leadership Actions: How Will You Help Me Get There?

Believing that role modeling is important ("not do as we say, but rather do as we do"), Dr. Stanford firmed up the Justice Academy's on-boarding process. All new faculty members are now required to successfully complete the Academy's General Instructor Training Course. This two-week course is designed for criminal justice personnel planning to teach in any course mandated by the Criminal Justice Education and Training Standards Commission or the Sheriff's Education and Training Standards Commission. This course provides information relating to instructional systems design and requires prospective trainers to successfully:

- Develop a lesson plan for an 80-minute block of instruction.
- Construct a test appropriate to the 80-minute block of instruction.
- Teach an 80-minute block of instruction.
- Complete a written examination.

The process is quite grueling. Prospective trainers must bring references and other materials necessary to enable them to research, write, type, and present the 80-minute block of instruction on a criminal justice-related topic. They typically spend two to three hours a night after their other classes are complete developing lesson plans and audiovisual aids, as well as preparing for their 80-minute presentation. However, this "boot camp" introduces newly appointed Justice Academy trainers to what is expected of them as they (1) personally prepare lesson plans and present them to colleagues for peer review and to managers for approval, and (2) present a block of instruction to students, either as a solo instructor or as part of an instructional team.

The General Instructor Training Course is only one example of how the Justice Academy sets and reinforces the standard against which all organizational members are expected to act. In addition to incorporating quality, service, and customer metrics into the academy's performance management system, Dr. Stanford considered the "eyes on" evaluation of instructors to be mission critical. As a result, all academy instructors receive periodic visits by their managers. These visits allow instructors to receive feedback not only from their students and peers but also from their managers on the quality of their lesson plans, the effectiveness of their instructional delivery, and the extent to which they recognize and respond to student needs throughout the block of instruction.

Although she found the Justice Academy to be a collegial environment, Dr. Stanford discovered there were no systems or programs in place to ease the initial transition period into the academy. Therefore she encouraged and supported the manager who created a formalized "buddy" system. New members of the organization now have someone to turn to for assistance and support when it comes to completing and submitting administrative forms, requisitioning supplies and equipment, and navigating the academy campus.

Dr. Stanford also found that the value the Justice Academy delivers lies in large part in the relevancy of its offerings. Students expect to successfully complete a Justice Academy–sponsored program and then be able to apply newly acquired/upgraded skills on return to their department. To help ensure the relevancy of its offerings, the Justice Academy now requires its instructors to seek out and accept annual 40-hour internships in positions similar to the ones that make up their student population. These internships are designed to sensitize academy faculty to the challenges and opportunities their students face, and in turn point them to the direction their courses and programs should take to remain relevant.

During the last 20 years, Dr. Stanford has stressed the importance of the Justice Academy remaining on the cutting edge, in terms of the courses and programs it offers and the technology it uses. As a result, the agency's strategic plan has periodically been reviewed and refined. Some technology has been abandoned while newer technologies have been adopted.

Numerous business processes have been streamlined and other business processes have been enhanced. A number of new initiatives are now offered to the North Carolina criminal justice community. The Justice Academy now sponsors a catalog of "Train-the-Trainer" courses, offers distance-learning courses and programs through Satellite TV and the Internet. In response to the needs and expectations of western North Carolina's criminal justice community, it now offers programs and courses at its newly opened Western Justice Academy.

Although Dr. Stanford has strived to maintain the Justice Academy's current path, the environment within which it functions has at times been quite turbulent. Economic pressures during the last 20 years have impacted government budgets. Dr. Stanford has had to lead the academy through several "no-growth" periods. Just as every other element of the criminal justice system was called on to respond to the September 11, 2001 attacks, so was the North Carolina Justice Academy. To address this need, it changed the courses and programs it offers, adapted the technical expertise it uses and the consultation it provides, and adjusted the level of security it offers its students, employees, and facilities. Throughout these and other challenges, academy faculty and staff note that Dr. Stanford addresses them with the criminal justice community's, the citizens', and their best interests in mind.

On the Justice Academy's twentieth anniversary, Dr. Stanford spearheaded an organizational renewal process. The process allowed the management team, key faculty, and staff to review the intent and purpose of the Justice Academy and to further determine how it might provide programs and work with other agencies to upgrade the North Carolina criminal justice system's practices and personnel. The formal mission statement and core values created during that process have helped the Justice Academy refocus on the importance of quality, service, and customer. The mission statement and core values are now a common theme of Dr. Stanford when addressing external stakeholders, reviewing the applications of prospective managers, faculty, and staff, and speaking to members of the organization.

After taking the North Carolina Justice Academy into the twenty-first century, and working with managers, faculty, and staff to refine the Academy's strategy, upgrade its technology, streamline and otherwise enhance its business processes, and introduce new initiatives to the criminal justice community, Dr. Stanford stresses the importance of the leader functioning in this context:

- Building self-awareness, in terms of what he or she expects and requires, and what he or she is willing to let go of;
- Taking the time to learn from internal and external stakeholders about what the organization is doing right and what it might do better;

- Communicating and reinforcing messages about the organization's mission and core values, and how members of the organization individually and as team members contribute to the organization's success;
- Communicating and reinforcing messages about how members of the organization are to treat each other and how they in turn can expect to be treated as they strive to accomplish the mission and perform in accordance to the core values;
- Taking the time to understand how various policies and practices impact the organization's ability to achieve its vision and to apply and modify those policies and practices as necessary to maximize achievement;
- Recognizing and celebrating—in different ways, at different times— the success of the organization and its team members;
- Monitoring the environment within which the organization functions and responding to unplanned events and circumstances in an appropriate way.

DISCUSSION QUESTIONS

1. What actions did Dr. Stanford display that typified the roles of custodial leader, trusting leader, nurturing leader, developmental leader, and supportive leader?
2. How were these roles integrated?
3. Which of these actions are most valuable to a leader being asked to move individuals along the current path or to otherwise maintain the organization's current state?

NINE

Receiving the Light: The Saga of the Uninvited Guest

We have all been one, seen one, or had to "deal" with one—the uninvited guest. Maybe it was a person at a wedding where neither side of the family seemed to know him or her. Perhaps it is how you felt when you entered a summer camp cabin or college dormitory for the first time only to find out you were the last one there and everyone else seemed to ignore you. Or it could have been when you stepped onto a bus or a train car, and no one would move their packages to give you a seat. You can even feel uninvited when you are simply trying to be alone. Did you ever take a walk through a park and get sidelong glances from couples strolling or families playing as they wondered if you were a threat to their safety or pleasure? In some of these instances you are even invited—it's just that it does not feel that way.

The saga of the uninvited guest happens all the time in organizations. It can occur when a new person joins an intact, high-performing team. It happens when a new worker joins others on the assembly line. It happens when a new leader enters an organization. You've heard, or maybe even said, the phrases:

- That's not how we do it here.
- That's not what the last person did.

- That's not what my old boss used to say.
- Where did you say you were from?
- How long are you planning to stay?

The challenge is to turn the reality, or the feeling, of not being invited into an invitation to join, and we mean really *join* the group.

So, if you feel uninvited, this is the section for you. If you are being asked as a new person to lead an organization along its current path, this section will provide advice on how to get a gold-plated invitation to lead.

DESCRIPTION OF THE SITUATION

The context of this section is that a leader new to the organization is required to maintain a current path or state for the organization. This could involve continuing to implement or maintaining a previously initiated or adopted strategy, technology, business process, or initiative. The leader may be completely new to the organization or may have worked for a number of years for a different part of the organization and be new to the current area he or she is being asked to lead. It is worth mentioning that organizational success takes more than effective implementation and maintenances practices—it requires continuous improvement.

INITIAL FOCUS OF THE LEADER

You have received the light of leadership from someone else. It was a light that may have been wielded well or poorly. Either way, the light is pointed in a direction that the people who invited you to lead want you to maintain.

Those who invited you have shown confidence in you by placing you in this leadership position. That does not mean, however, that they have no doubts about your abilities or that their confidence will endure regardless of your actions. You will need to strive to enhance your credibility and ensure them that you will, in fact, lead in the desired direction.

Those you will be leading are just getting to know you. They may have liked or disliked the previous leader. Either way, they were following him or her in the direction they were being led. You will need to work to gain their confidence that you have bought into the organization's direction and you will have to strive to gain credibility and ensure they will follow your leadership. To solidify and broaden your "invitation," you will need to emphasize five leadership roles.

PRIMARY ROLE EMPHASIS

If you have received the leadership light from someone else and are being asked to maintain the current direction, we recommend that you work to: (1) give others confidence that you will support the current direction and (2) get people to respect your role as a leader. This can be accomplished by emphasizing the following five leadership roles:

- Custodial leader
- Trusted leader
- Trusting leader
- Developmental leader
- Supportive leader

Your initial emphasis should be to demonstrate your desire to lead the organization down its current path by emphasizing the role of custodial leader. Also, focus initially on the roles of trusted leader and trusting leader to gain credibility. Establishing these roles will allow you to use the roles of supportive leader to help your followers accomplish their goals and developmental leader to make certain they have the required skill sets to be successful in the near term and long term. How to apply these roles, as well as suggested actions, are described next.

Why Should I Follow You?—Custodial Leader, Trusted Leader, and Trusting Leader

Maintaining the current path or state as a new leader to the organization suggests maintaining over the long term. There are three key reasons why people in this context will follow you:

- They have confidence that you will continue to lead them down the currently successful path.
- They trust you.
- They believe that you trust them.

Above all else, the custodial leader strives to sustain momentum using actions that drive and support the organization's vision and key values for the long term and makes certain the light of leadership never burns out. The custodial leader must do all that he or she can on a daily basis to ensure immediate and short-term success and, in doing so, must keep in the back of his or her mind that all leadership decisions and actions will influence and otherwise contribute to the organization's future success. In the end, the custodial leader must recognize that his or her decisions and actions will ultimately impact the organization that he or she leaves behind, including the organization's vision, strategies, technology, business processes, initiatives, and people.

When you are trying to get an organization to maintain its current path or its organizational state, your biggest enemy may be repetitiveness and the resulting boredom and lack of creativity. Within such a context, you must constantly and consistently point out what is truly important and how what each and every member of the organization does on a daily basis impacts the organization in a positive or negative (and very seldom, in a neutral) way. To heighten and/or reinforce your continued and constant desire to lead the organization down its current path, consider the appropriateness of the following actions of the custodial leader:

- Focus on what has fueled past success.
- Ensure a constant flow of leadership talent.
- Consider the long-term impact of your actions.
- Consider your impact on the environment.
- Ensure creative and innovative ideas are celebrated, not simply tolerated.
- Ensure that key challenges and triumphs are remembered.
- Identify the organization's heroes and ensure that their stories are known by all.
- Record the "whys" of decisions so that they can be archived for future reference.
- Ensure that today's strengths are applied to future challenges and opportunities.
- Protect what has transcended past generations and must transcend future generations.
- Strive to sustain the organization for the long term.

Whereas the role of the custodial leader will help convince people that you are willing to lead others down the current path, the role of trusted leader will help you begin to establish yourself as someone people are willing to follow. Honesty and consistency of your actions and words will go a long way toward winning the confidence of followers. This is true whether you are keeping promises as simple as starting a meeting on time or when you are being open and honest about your mistakes (as the person learning the direction, others already know you *will* make mistakes).

The role of the trusted leader is also necessary to strike the appropriate balance between an organization maintaining the current path and an organization responding to unforeseen and unplanned forces. Operating in today's turbulent business environment, leaders recognize that the "space" within which the organization functions must be closely monitored, and the organization's strategic plan (and thus, the full gamut of its will and resources) must quickly change to respond to unforeseen and unplanned situations and circumstances. In today's environment, business as usual can quickly become business as unusual. Today's leader must therefore reinforce to his or her followers that if or when the organization's path needs to change, they can have the confidence that the leader will be there to lead them to the new destination. Seek out opportunities to earn the trust of your people by taking the following actions of the trusted leader:

- Tell the truth, the whole truth, and nothing but the truth.
- Lead by example.
- Admit your mistakes.
- Collaborate with others.
- Keep your promises.
- Spend time building people up instead of tearing them down.
- Consider the needs of others first.
- Consistently be open and honest, even when it "hurts."
- Ask those closest to you to take the same risks you are asking of others.
- Advocate for your people.
- Share your fears.
- Assess your intentions.
- Accurately communicate the opinions of others even when you disagree.
- Be consistent in your actions.

In this context, the role of trusting leader is the third way to get people to follow you. As a leader, you expect people to trust you. From their perspective, why should they trust you if you don't trust them? After all, they are the ones that have been making the organization succeed in its current direction. To gain the trust of your followers, you must demonstrate that you trust them. As you work to get people to respect your leadership, consider the following actions of the trusting leader:

- Allow others to lead.
- Give others permission to make mistakes.
- Reinforce good performance.
- Celebrate the achievement of others.
- Give authority to people to whom you have given responsibility.
- Do not punish the bearer of bad news.
- Act on others' ideas when appropriate.
- Seek ideas from others.
- Focus on the goal and let others worry about the how.
- When appropriate, act on the advice of others, even when you strongly disagree with them.

- Recognize that people's fears are their realities.
- Trust others enough to share your leadership responsibilities.

Where Are You Leading Me? Trusting Leader

The role of the trusting leader can help you solidify confidence others have in your leadership, but it can also serve another purpose. When there is clarity around the direction the organization is headed and people are successfully making that journey, you have the opportunity to further engage people in refining the strategies and tactics for achieving the direction. This will serve to further solidify understanding of the vision allowing members of the organization to constantly monitor the situation to determine what can be altered to improve execution of the current direction. This allows you and your organization to continue to build on previous successes by continuously improving what everyone is doing.

When engaging others in helping refine what you need to do to continue to succeed, consider the following actions of the trusted leader:

- Allow others to lead.
- Give others permission to make mistakes.
- Reinforce good performance.
- Celebrate the achievement of others.
- Give authority to people to whom you have given responsibility.
- Act on others' ideas when appropriate.
- Seek ideas from others.
- Focus on the goal and let others worry about the how.
- When appropriate, act on the advice of others, even when you strongly disagree with them.
- Trust others enough to share your leadership responsibilities.

How Will You Help Me Get There? Developmental Leader and Supportive Leader

Once you have created a good "enabling" relationship with your followers, you then need to take steps to ensure that they have the knowledge, skills, and abilities needed to most fully contribute to the organization's vision and mission. This is accomplished by emphasizing the role of the developmental leader. The developmental leader ensures that no opportunities need be missed. This includes an individual not missing an opportunity because of lack of personal development and the organization not missing an opportunity due to an absence of the necessary knowledge and skills. Consider the following actions as you emphasize the role of the developmental leader:

- Give people the chance to learn from others' expertise.
- In addition to celebrating successes, share "lessons" with others so that they, too, may learn from your experiences.
- Give people a chance to discover how to accomplish their objectives.
- Find out what people have to contribute.
- Solicit input from others.
- Give others the opportunity to plot the path forward.
- Allow people to contribute the expertise they have collected from other experiences.
- Ask others their perception of what your role should be.
- Give people the chance to examine their challenges from a different perspective.
- Challenge the group so they think in more creative and innovative ways.
- Give people an opportunity for broader experiences.
- Understand the capabilities of your group.

Successful organizations, even those maintaining the current path, rely on the achievements of their people to accomplish and produce optimal results. Otherwise, they do not deliver on the expectations set forth in their mission statement, nor are they likely to attain their vision. This is why it is crucial that the leader *support* those striving to maintain the current path. As you emphasize the role of the supportive leader, consider the following actions:

- Make certain that people are linked together in their efforts.
- Make certain that people who need extra support get it.
- Reassure people that they will have access to what they need to succeed.
- Set a pace to allow everyone to "keep up."
- Provide people with a comprehensive view of the destination and the obstacles and challenges.
- Clarify the process for moving forward and ensuring everyone's success.
- Personally sacrifice for the "common" good in times of extreme crisis.
- Make certain the workload is balanced for everyone.
- Make certain you have sufficiently budgeted to allow new ideas to be fully and thoroughly implemented.
- Consistently communicate key messages to all areas and levels of the organization.
- Empower people to take action.
- Reorganize your teams for more effective performance.
- Give people sufficient time to try their ideas.

SECONDARY ROLE EMPHASIS

Although important, certain roles may need to receive secondary emphasis when maintaining the current direction. These roles are:

- Nurturing leader
- Working leader

Nurturing Leader: Solidifying Why I Should Follow You

A portion of your followers may need additional assurance that they should follow you. You may have convinced them you will keep the organization on its current course, but they may not yet believe that you are interested in their personal success. Seek out opportunities to continue to build others' confidence in your leadership by taking the following actions of the nurturing leader:

- Work to establish a sense of "family" within your organization.
- Regularly check how everyone is doing emotionally, psychologically, and physically.
- Learn from your direct reports, encouraging them to share their skills.
- Focus your attention on the immediate needs of the people.
- Focus your attention on calming the fears of people.
- Strive to understand and reduce the limitations of others.
- Spend time helping people get "little doses" of the challenges facing them.
- Ensure the voice of the minority is heard and taken into consideration.
- Focus on people's development.
- Take steps to ensure that people are proud of how they are developing.
- Show individuals the progress they are making.
- Be honest about people's abilities when you focus on developing people.

Working Leader: Solidifying How You Will Help Me Get There

To ensure the organization's future success, you must actively engage people in addressing the challenges of the present. This is accomplished by emphasizing the role of the working leader. In maintaining the current direction, people should already understand where they are headed and how they are to get there. Use the role of the working leader with teams or people who need help focusing on what their priorities should be or how their work needs to be done. Also, use this role to reinforce how people are to think, behave, and act toward others while working toward achieving the desired results. Be cautious; if you place too much emphasis on this role early in your tenure with the organization, people may view your actions as an indication that you do not trust them to do their jobs.

Consider the following actions as you emphasize the role of the working leader:

- Work among—and with—others to solve problems.
- Monitor, measure, and communicate progress.
- Make certain you adequately supply people with the tools they need.
- Help people differentiate between crises and mere inconveniences.
- Let people know that you are open to suggestions and recommendations.
- Devote time to accurately assess the contributions you make as "Leader."
- At the end of the day, review today's actions and plan for tomorrow.
- Focus on the details.
- Balance "hard" and "soft" measures.
- Remain mentally agile and apply personal creativity to the situation at hand.

ADDITIONAL ROLES

Certain actions within the roles of strategic leader and inspiring leader may also contribute to your success within this context. While focusing on the primary and secondary roles, capitalize on opportunities to exhibit these actions:

Strategic Leader
- Share what you see with others.
- Accept input from other sources.
- Show people the boundaries within which they operate.
- Focus everyone's attention on where you are going.
- Help others focus on the overall mission rather than on the day-to-day challenges and crises.
- Keep an eye on the competition.
- Try to see things from a different perspective.
- Learn more about your industry.

Inspiring Leader

- Show people how close they are to reaching their destination.
- Reinforce that people are not alone in the challenges they face and that everyone will share together in the eventual rewards.
- Remind people of the dream that started them out on this journey.
- Remind people that, by working together, any obstacles will be easily overcome.
- Remind people of what they have accomplished so far.
- Remind people they have already overcome much more challenging situations.
- Exhibit the confidence and drive needed to inspire others.
- Find out what your people do best and link it to the dream.
- Give people the opportunity to do what they do best, in pursuit of the dream.
- Articulate your dream, along with the dreams of the organization.
- Spend time encouraging others.

WHEN IT'S TIME TO CHANGE THE LEADERSHIP ROLE EMPHASIS

There are three triggers that require you to consider shifting your emphasis on the five primary leadership roles: (1) people begin to look around for additional challenges, or other factors combine to require you to set a new direction, (2) progress begins to bog down, and (3) the organizational context significantly changes.

If people begin to look around for additional challenges, or if other factors combine to require you to set a new direction, consider continuing to focus on the five primary roles while directing time and energy toward the role of strategic leader:

- Share what you see with others.
- Accept input from other sources.
- Show people the boundaries within which they operate.
- Focus everyone's attention on where you are going.
- Help others focus on the overall mission rather than on the day-to-day challenges and crises.
- Keep an eye on the competition.
- Try to see things from a different perspective.

If progress begins to bog down and if momentum waivers, consider moving away from the custodial leader, trusting leader, and developmental leader roles and place additional emphasis on the working leader and inspiring leader roles.

If the organization context significantly changes, consider moving away from the current leadership behaviors toward those that more closely match the new organizational context (which are described elsewhere in this section).

IN PRACTICE

As we were conducting our research and formulating advice to share with leaders, the opportunity to apply our model to a real-world situation surfaced. This is our story.

The Scenario

The First Congregational Church, UCC of Sheboygan, Wisconsin, is the oldest church in the city. Founded in 1845, its members over the years have proven to be good stewards of the church—spiritually and facility-wise. Their first church building was dedicated in 1847. Over the next 157 years, the congregation was asked on seven different occasions to upgrade, renovate, or rebuild the facilities. This work included building two new churches, moving an existing church, remodeling parts of the buildings, repairing extensive damage stemming from two separate fires, and building a fellowship hall. A pipe organ is a significant monetary investment and the congregation has also purchased two organs over the years: the first one in 1890 and a second one in 1960.

The current pipe organ started failing in 2001. The church hired an organ consultant to help them decide what to do about the organ. The consultant recommended that the organ be replaced and that acoustical work be done on the sanctuary to enhance the musical and worship experience. Committees were formed to address the organ issue and to determine what other construction would be done to repair or enhance the church's facilities.

Committee members worked diligently and as quickly as they could, given the volunteer nature of their positions. The Organ Committee had to answer the following questions:

- Should we repair or replace the organ?
- If we replace the organ, should we purchase a pipe organ, a digital organ, or a combination of the two?
- If we purchase an organ, should we place it in the back (the organ's current location) or front of the church?

In December 2002, and again in January 2003, the Organ Committee shared information with the congregation. At an official Congregational Meeting in March 2003, the Organ Committee submitted their recommendation: purchase a new pipe organ and place it in the rear of the church. A directional-only vote was held and the congregation voted to support the direction the Organ Committee was taking and authorize it to obtain bids. There was broad support for this direction (156 Yes, 8 No, 1 Undecided), but several members of the congregation voiced the opinion that there were other needs around the world that far outweighed the need for the congregation to spend such a significant amount of money on a new organ. Also, as this vote was directional only, no one knew how people would vote when actually asked to pledge money to support the purchase of a new organ.

The spring and summer of 2003 were busy. The Organ Committee met with several organ builders and visited churches to hear music played on various types of organs. Another committee, the Building Renovation Committee, was also hard at work identifying needs and gathering data. A Capital Campaign Finance Committee was formed to make decisions around how to lead the financial campaign needed for such a large project. Both the congregation's lack of experience in raising funds of this magnitude for a capital campaign and the economic impact of the September 11, 2001 terrorist attacks compelled the Finance Committee to consider using a consultant with expertise in conducting capital campaigns for religious institutions. Early conversations with consultants indicated that—given recent stewardship trends in the church—securing adequate funding for the new organ and the desired building renovations would be challenging. This potential challenge was verified in February 2004, when results of a feasibility study conducted in November 2003 were delivered to the congregation.

Cost figures for the renovations were shared with the congregation and architectural drawings were displayed throughout the fall of 2003. Two informal meetings were held in January 2004; interested parties were given the opportunity to provide feedback on the organ and renovation recommendations.

At the end of January 2004, Mike Venn was invited to serve as church moderator for the congregation. The church moderator is the lay leader of the church and serves a one-year term heading the church council (the governing board of the church). Venn was a relatively new member of a church that prides itself in the number of people who have been members for more than 50 years. Venn had served one year as a member of the church council and one year as vice moderator. The church had a practice of the moderator and vice moderator working as a team to ensure a smooth exchange of leadership from year-to-year.

In most years the role of church moderator is not very visible to the average church member. The moderator presides over monthly council meetings and the church's annual meeting. However, the behind-the-scenes work can keep the moderator busy throughout the year. The moderator for the prior year had been more visible than most primarily due to the congregational and information meetings surrounding the potential capital campaign. This need for increased visibility would continue into and throughout the year of Venn's tenure.

Leadership Actions: Why Should I Follow You?

Venn held the post of moderator, but the reality was that he was one of several leaders within the church. The church had a senior minister and a minister of education. There were three church officers (moderator, vice moderator, and treasurer). In addition to the church council, there were nine boards or committees, each with a chairperson. For the potential capital campaign, there were three active committees, each with a chairperson. The church was running well and the campaign committees were hard at work.

In the first half of the year, Venn spoke to the congregation on several occasions to inform members of the progress being made on the capital campaign. He also capitalized on numerous opportunities to have conversations with individuals. In all of these interactions he worked hard to provide accurate information and always supported the recommendations of the various committees. He also listened to the opinions voiced to him and, when appropriate, shared that information with appropriate committees. He was honest about what information was known, what was not known, and when additional information would be available.

People voiced concerns about what would happen if they voted to fund all of the projects but then could not raise enough money to fund them all. Venn, along with others, continued to reinforce the message that nothing would occur without the vote and endorsement of the entire congregation. Venn emphasized that if the congregation voted to hold a capital campaign for all of the projects and, at the end of the campaign the money pledged was not sufficient to fund all of the projects, then the congregation would be allowed to determine which projects would and would not be funded. Venn stressed that he too was concerned about the large amount of money that was needed, but that he had faith that the finances would work out as long as the congregation moved down the path it felt was right.

Leadership Actions: Where Are You Leading Me?

When Venn assumed the role of moderator, the capital campaign was set to address three areas: the organ purchase, building renovations, and mission (later changed to endowment fund). There were still three issues at play around the direction this project was taking. First, different areas were more or less important to different individuals. This led to several members of the congregation speaking out against certain parts of the campaign, not because they felt those elements were wrong, but because they felt they were not as important as one or more of the other areas of the campaign. Second, people were beginning to get worn down because of the length of the debate. Third, there were a small number of people who strongly believed that one or more of the areas should not be funded.

Findings of the feasibility study were reported to the church council in February 2004. The study suggested that there were some unanswered questions about the capital campaign and a lack of awareness on the part of some people. The study concluded that additional information was needed and that information needed to be more effectively communicated; however, Venn realized it was time to draw a line in the sand. The church council met with members of the three committees, described what additional information needed to be gathered, laid out some aggressive timelines, and advised the committees that the council would endorse the committees' final recommendations and take the entire matter before the congregation for a vote.

Leadership Actions: How Will You Help Me Get There?

In May 2004, the church council accepted the recommendations of all three committees. With that step completed, the council hired a campaign consultant. With confidence that the committee had recommended the right consultant to help the church, council members spent time reassuring each other that everyone needed to trust him and follow his advice.

As preparations were made for a June congregational vote, the council understood there were still dissenting viewpoints within the congregation. The council therefore decided to discuss how it would conduct the open meeting, facilitate the discussion, and hold the vote with the congregation. The consultant suggested that an 80 percent positive vote was necessary to conduct a successful capital campaign. The council realized that some portion of the congregation would inevitably vote on the losing side. Foremost on the minds of Venn and the entire council was the desire to maintain the unity of the congregation. During the formal congregational meeting it would be important for all viewpoints to be heard. A member of the church with expertise in parliamentary procedures was therefore asked to serve as parliamentarian during the meeting to ensure rules that support the open exchange of viewpoints would be followed.

Venn and others working for the campaign held countless conversations. They worked to instill confidence that although the congregation had not recently taken on an effort of such magnitude, they *had* successfully done so on nine previous occasions in the church's 160-year history. Venn dealt with the fears of some by helping them understand that, if sufficient pledges were not raised to fund all aspects of the capital campaign, the entire congregation, not some small committee, would determine which components of the campaign would be undertaken. Until that failure occurred, Venn encouraged people to have confidence that the congregation was doing what was right for the church and that chances for success were high.

In preparing to put the capital campaign before the congregation for a vote, many council and campaign committee members stayed after church on successive Sundays to hold informal question-and-answer sessions with anyone who was interested. All involved worked to listen intently, inform accurately, and share with each other what they learned. Also, in early June the church held an "All Boards Night" where anyone serving on a church board or committee—or anyone else who was interested—was invited to discuss and share their thoughts on:

1. How the church and its mission had been strengthened throughout the past year
2. How the capital campaign might strengthen the church for generations to come
3. Other things the congregation might do to strengthen the church

In mid-June 2004, the congregational meeting was held. There was much conversation on both sides of the issues, questions were asked and answered, and finally the vote was taken. The capital campaign was endorsed by 82 percent of the congregation. Now the real work began—conducting the campaign.

On the advice of the consultant, the council involved as many people as possible in the campaign. A theme was selected: "Honoring our past, building our future." Education sessions were held where Venn and the moderator from 2003 shared additional information about the campaign with members of the congregation. More than 40 people spent many hours visiting church members, sharing additional information about the campaign and its goals, and challenging members with a suggested pledge amount.

The work finally came to an end in January 2005, the pledges were in and tallied, and the result was announced. With a goal to raise $1,074,992, the church had received pledges totaling $1,313,299.60! There was still plenty of work to do, but church members paused long enough to celebrate their success.

As Venn reflects back on his experiences, he considers the following to be valuable advice for others trying to lead in this context:

- Trust the people around you.
- Respect the work of those who led before you.
- Try to understand people's fears.
- Work to calm the fears of others.
- Always be straightforward and honest—publicly and privately.
- Communicate, communicate, communicate—and then communicate some more.
- Continue to remind people *why* we are going down this path.
- If you believe in the path, believe in the people to successfully navigate the path.

DISCUSSION QUESTIONS

1. What actions did Venn and others display that typified the roles of custodial leader, trusting leader, trusted leader, developmental leader, and supportive leader?
2. How were these roles integrated?
3. Which of the actions are most valuable to maintain a current path or state as the new leader?

You now recognize the important role context plays in your professional life and to the importance of your thinking and acting as a contextual leader. While Chapters 4–9 provide information on numerous roles, actions, and behaviors you must consider as you strive to be successful in your context, Chapter 10 provides detailed information on the competencies that underlie those roles, actions, and behaviors.

PART III

Action Plan, Tools, and Resources

TEN

Skills and Competencies

The best of us and the worst of us all have room for improvement. The previous chapters offer numerous roles, actions, and behaviors for you to consider as you strive to succeed in your context. Underpinning all of these roles, actions, and behaviors are competencies.

We consider competencies to be actions and behaviors (grouped together in like categories) that enable you to succeed in your current role. An understanding of how effectively you exhibit various competencies can be invaluable in your developing personal leadership capabilities and to your using those capabilities to improve the performance of your organization.

Having worked with various human resources organizations, we understand the value and usefulness of competencies and the need to assess your effectiveness against competencies. After we completed the Contextual Leadership Model, our next task was to describe the behaviors and actions in terms of competencies. This can be a rather daunting task because of the complexity of describing comprehensive yet discrete behaviors for every competency. We chose a path of partnering with:

- Bigby, Havis & Associates, Inc., leading experts in psychometric measurement who have defined competencies and developed psy-

chometric tools to measure individual performance against those
competencies
- Peak Performance Associates, a national distributor of Bigby, Havis
  & Associates, Inc. products who possess expertise in mapping roles,
  behaviors, and actions against competencies

Our partnership with Bigby, Havis & Associates, Inc. and Peak Performance Associates led to the identification of 23 competencies important
for the contextual leader.

The following competencies map to the roles, behaviors, and actions
that make up the Contextual Leadership Model. The definitions for each
of the competencies come from the Bigby, Havis & Associates, Inc. AS-
SESS360° Multirater Report (as listed in the Contextual Leadership Model
report):[1]

Business Acumen—Understanding general business and financial
concepts, understanding the company's business, and using both
general and specific knowledge to be effective. People who display this competency will have a good understanding of general
business and financial concepts. They are effective at using this
knowledge to understand important business issues related to
their work.

Championing Change—Taking action to support and implement change
initiatives effectively. People who display this competency actively
lead change efforts through their words, as well as their actions.
They build the support of those affected by the change initiative and
take personal responsibility to ensure that changes are successfully
implemented.

Coaching and Developing Others—Advising, assisting, mentoring, and providing feedback to others to encourage and inspire the development
of work-related competencies and long-term career growth. People
who display this competency are sincerely interested in the development and success of others. They provide honest feedback and guidance in a supportive manner and assist others in meeting individual
goals and challenges. In all, they are positive, objective, and fair.

Conflict Management—Managing conflict between people and effectively
resolving sensitive issues. People who are competent at managing
conflict are objective, fair, and tactful. They bring issues into the
open, work to understand both perspectives, seek common ground,
and work to find a resolution that is satisfactory to all.

Continuous Learning—Striving to expand knowledge and refine skills
through education and training. Inspiring others to develop and
refine knowledge and skills relevant to their work. People who dis-

play this competency always strive to improve their knowledge, understanding, abilities, and skills throughout their working lives. Through their example or by direct encouragement, they also inspire others to be lifelong learners.

Courage of Convictions—Having the personal courage to address difficult issues in the face of potential opposition. People who display this competency place a high importance on addressing difficult issues. They are willing to say and do what they think is right, even when others around them have a different perspective.

Customer Focus—Anticipating customers' needs and designing, promoting, or supporting the delivery of products and services that exceed customers' expectations. People who are competent at customer focus have a desire to please customers and seek to anticipate customers' needs. They push the organization to do more than is required to ensure that the customer is satisfied.

Driving for Results—Challenging, pushing the organization and themselves to excel and achieve. People who exhibit a drive for results establish or help establish objectives and contribute to their accomplishment. They assume personal responsibility for the success of the organization and persist, even when faced with obstacles, to achieve results.

In-Depth Problem Solving and Analysis—Solving difficult problems through careful and systematic evaluation of information, possible alternatives, and consequences. People who are competent at in-depth problem solving and analysis are capable of generating good solutions to difficult problems. They consider many sources of information, systematically process and evaluate the information against possible courses of action, and carefully deliberate before a final decision is made.

Influencing and Persuading—Convincing others to adopt a course of action. People who display this competency influence others without being excessively aggressive or pushy. They understand their audience and modify their method of persuasion accordingly. They are confident and do not give up easily.

Integrity—Upholding a high standard of fairness and ethics in everyday words and actions. People who display this competency conscientiously and reliably behave in an ethical and honest manner in their dealings with management, peers, direct reports, and customers. They are fair in their expectations of others and behave toward others with equal fairness.

Interpersonal Communication—Communicating clearly and effectively with people inside and outside the organization. People who are competent at interpersonal communication listen effectively and develop rapport with others. They are able to articulate their thoughts and ideas clearly, they present information in a straightforward and logical way, and they ensure that they are understood. They share information with others that will improve overall work progress.

Managing Others—Directing and leading others to accomplish organizational goals and objectives. People who display this competency effectively manage and direct the activities of others. They work through other people to accomplish objectives, and they encourage performance through motivation and feedback. They hold people accountable.

Motivating Others—Inspiring others to perform well by actively conveying enthusiasm and a passion for doing a good job. People who display this competency encourage and inspire others.

Organizational Savvy—Recognizing and understanding organizational politics and working within organizational dynamics to accomplish objectives. People who exhibit organizational savvy understand the social and political dynamics within an organization and build and maintain partnerships and alliances. They understand people's roles in the organization and can effectively work through others to get needed resources and accomplish objectives.

Planning and Organizing—Effectively organizing and planning work according to organizational needs by defining objectives and anticipating needs and priorities. People who are competent at planning and organizing efficiently manage their time and the time of others and effectively handle multiple demands and competing deadlines. They identify goals, develop plans, estimate time frames, and monitor progress.

Presentation Skills—Having the skills to effectively communicate to an audience in a formal setting. People who display this competency are able to organize and articulate their thoughts and ideas clearly. They use visual presentation tools to deliver information in a straightforward and logical way. They prepare well, adjust their message to their audience, and deliver smoothly.

Relationship Management—Developing and maintaining positive relationships with individuals outside their work group. People who are competent at relationship management actively seek opportunities to build relationships important to their business. They are in frequent contact with internal or external customers to ensure satisfaction. They consider how their actions or decisions may impact other groups or departments and work collaboratively to accomplish work goals.

Resilience—Effectively dealing with work-related problems, pressure, and stress in a professional and positive manner. People who exhibit resilience maintain a positive attitude even when faced with frustration, pressure, or change. They recover quickly when faced with obstacles or setbacks.

Respecting Diversity—Understanding, accepting, and being sensitive to individual differences. Treating all people equally, regardless of gender, race, creed, place of origin, status, or level of position. People who display this competency are open and accepting of the richness of differences among people. They treat others fairly and with dignity.

Teamwork and Collaboration—Effectively working and collaborating with others toward a common goal. People who are competent at teamwork build and maintain cooperative work relationships with others. They complete their own tasks for group projects in a timely and responsible manner and directly contribute to reaching the group goal.

Visioning—Identifying long-term goals and championing the implementation of different or alternative ideas. People who are competent at visioning generate creative and strategic solutions that can be successfully implemented. They think in innovative ways and support similar thinking in others. They challenge and push the organization to constantly improve and grow.

Written Communication—Having the skills to communicate to others in a written format. People who are competent in written communication are able to organize and articulate their thoughts well in formal and informal writings. They adjust their message, vocabulary, and form of writing to best speak to their audience.

As with the leadership roles, the competencies you emphasize should depend on the context in which you are leading. The next chapter helps you identify competencies that are important for your immediate success.

ELEVEN

Diagnosis

The Contextual Leadership Model ties the nine leadership roles and associated competencies outlined in Chapter 3 to the six organizational contexts described in Chapters 4 through 9. Whereas more traditional approaches to leadership and leadership development suggest that you should apply the same (or similar) leadership actions across all situations and circumstances, the power of the Contextual Leadership Model is that it allows you to (1) crystallize your understanding of the assumptions and expectations your particular circumstances bring with them and (2) apply specific leadership roles, behaviors, actions, and competencies to address those particular assumptions and expectations.

To maximize leadership performance and to optimize the extent to which you influence your followers, you must determine the context within which you function and decide which leadership roles and associated competencies to emphasize. To personally grow and to further develop your leadership abilities—and to do so in an effective and efficient manner—you must target three or four areas that, if further developed, are most likely to impact your success as a leader given the context within which you function.

Such an approach to leadership and leadership development cannot occur in an ad hoc or haphazard way; it must be both planned and purposeful. We therefore recommend that, whether preparing to function as a leader or taking steps to further develop your leadership skills, you first diagnose your situation. In this diagnosis we recommend that you consider the expectations of your organization stakeholders, culture, and practices. This chapter provides a process and tools you can use to diagnose:

- Your leadership context
- Which of the nine leadership roles to emphasize
- Actions and behaviors within those roles on which you should focus your leadership light
- Competencies you should further develop and leverage

DIAGNOSING YOUR LEADERSHIP CONTEXT

Review the following descriptions of the six organizational contexts and consider which one most closely describes the context within which you are being asked to manage. Your selection will reflect your personal opinion; however, it should be based on information and direction you have received from the board, influential stakeholders, and/or senior leadership.

✓ Start Up a New Organization (Could Be New Business, Department, or Functional Area)
Tasks: May involve establishing a successful strategy, adopting new technology, or designing and implementing new business processes and initiatives.
Focus:

- On the new vision
- Establishing the right culture
- Creating a high-performing team (with a sense of community)
- Getting everyone moving in the right direction
- Establishing the foundation for your personal success
- Gaining the support you need to begin making substantial progress
- The need to plot the path forward
- Laying the groundwork for organizational success

✓ Take an Organization in a New Direction from a Successful State When People Are Open to Change
Tasks: May involve adopting a new strategy or business model, introducing new technologies, and designing or implementing new business processes and initiatives.
Focus:

- On the new vision
- Plotting the new path forward
- Getting everyone moving in the new direction
- Redirecting the momentum of your organization
- *Retaining* a critical mass of followers
- Alleviating concerns pertaining to changes in your focus, actions, and behavior
- Ensuring the ongoing support you need to achieve your new direction
- Establishing the groundwork for organizational success

✓ Take an Organization in a New Direction from a Successful State When People Are Resistant to Change
Tasks: May involve adopting a new strategy or business model, introducing new technologies, and designing or implementing new business processes and initiatives.
Focus:

- On the new vision
- Plotting the new path forward
- Getting everyone moving in the new direction
- Redirecting the momentum of your organization
- *Attaining* a critical mass of followers
- Alleviating concerns pertaining to changes in your focus, actions, and behavior
- Attaining the support you need to achieve your new direction
- Establishing the groundwork for organizational success

✓ Take an Organization in a New Direction from a Failed State
Tasks: Replace a failed strategy, technology, business process, or initiative; or lead a complete business turnaround.
Focus:

- Establishing your direction
- *Quickly plotting* the new path forward
- Getting everyone *quickly* moving in the new direction
- Gaining a critical mass of followers

- Gaining access to the support you need to achieve your new direction
- Establishing the groundwork for success

✓ Maintain a Current Path/State
Tasks: Maintain the current strategy, technology, business process, and initiatives.
Focus:
- Taking steps to maintain and enhance the state you have established within the organization
- Ensuring that others are following your leadership
- Taking steps to ensure that people continue respecting your role as a leader
- Giving others confidence that you will continue supporting the current direction of the organization
- Helping your followers accomplish their goals
- Making certain your followers have the required skill sets to be successful in the near term and long term.

✓ New Person Required to Maintain a Current Path/State
Tasks: Continue implementing or maintaining a successful strategy, technology, business process, or initiative.
Focus:
- Gaining credibility within the organization
- Getting people to begin following your leadership
- Giving others the confidence that you will support the current direction of the organization
- Gaining the respect you need in your leadership role
- Demonstrating your desire to lead the organization down its current path
- Helping your followers accomplish their goals
- Making certain your team members have the required skill sets to be successful in the near term and long term.

DIAGNOSING WHICH LEADERSHIP
ROLES TO EMPHASIZE

The Contextual Leadership Model suggests that you should think, behave, and perform in a way that matches needs and expectations associated with the context within which you manage. You must therefore focus on the vital few leadership roles most likely to address the needs and expectations before you and thusly most likely to allow you to influence your followers to (1) perform at exemplary levels and (2) achieve what they otherwise might have considered impossible.

Using your analysis of the above six contexts in the previous section, place an "X" next to the organizational context that best describes your situation and review the advice for that context:

- ✓ Start Up a New Organization—First establish your role as a *nurturing leader* and *trusted leader*. Once these "enabling" roles are adequately established, you will have access to the support you need to be successful in additional roles. Emphasizing the role of *strategic leader* gives you the viewpoint you need to plot the path forward, and emphasizing the role of *working leader* helps you establish the groundwork for success.
- ✓ Take an Organization in a New Direction from a Successful State When People Are Open to Change—As you consider a new direction, you must emphasize the role of *custodial leader* to protect what has contributed to current (and prior) success. Given that you are heading in a new direction from a successful state where people are open to change, you can emphasize the *trusting leader* role and engage others in designing the new direction. Once you have established this "enabling role," you will be assured the ongoing support you need to achieve your new direction. Emphasizing the role of *strategic leader* gives you the viewpoint you need to plot the new path forward, and emphasizing the role of *supportive leader* helps establish the groundwork for success.
- ✓ Take an Organization in a New Direction from a Successful State When People Are Resistant to Change—Change in emphasis and direction will create doubt concerning the consistency of your actions and behavior; you must therefore reinforce your role of *trusted leader*. Once you have adequately reinforced this "enabling" role, you will be ensured the ongoing support you need to achieve your new direction. Emphasizing the role of *strategic leader* gives you the viewpoint you need to plot the new path forward and emphasizing the roles of *working leader* and *supportive leader* help establish the groundwork for success.
- ✓ Take an Organization in a New Direction from a Failed State—You must first establish your role of *trusted leader*. Once this "enabling" role is adequately established, you will have access to the support you need to be successful in additional roles. Emphasizing the role of *strategic leader* gives you the viewpoint you need to plot the path forward. Emphasizing the roles of *working leader* and *supportive leader* helps establish the groundwork for success.
- ✓ Maintain a Current Path/State—Absent the obvious need for additional emphasis in one or more leadership roles, you must give others

confidence that you will continue to support the current direction of the organization and take steps to ensure that people continue respecting your role as a leader. Your emphasis should be on maintaining or enhancing the role of *custodial leader* to demonstrate the continued and constant desire to lead the organization down its current path. Also, focus on the roles of *trusting leader* and *nurturing leader* to reinforce credibility. Once these roles are adequately reinforced, continue to use the role of *supportive leader* to help your followers accomplish their goals and *developmental leader* to make certain they have the required skill sets to be successful in the near term and long term.

✓ New Person Required to Maintain a Current Path/State—Your initial emphasis should be on establishing the role of *custodial leader* to demonstrate your desire to lead the organization down its current path. Also, focus initially on the roles of *trusted leader* and *trusting leader* to gain credibility. Establishing these roles will allow you to use the roles of *supportive leader* to help your followers accomplish their goals and *developmental leader* to make certain they have the required skill sets to be successful in the near term and long term.

DIAGNOSING LEADERSHIP ACTIONS AND BEHAVIORS ON WHICH TO FOCUS

Using the information in the previous section, we recommend that you identify a few (again, no more than three or four) leadership roles on which to focus. Two caveats are in order:

- If you are functioning as a leader, your challenge will be to seek out and capitalize on opportunities to exhibit these behaviors on a daily basis.
- If you are attempting to further develop your leadership skills, your challenge will be to seek out and capitalize on leadership development offerings which allow you to develop, test, and practice (in a safe way) these particular leadership behaviors.

As you select the leadership roles from the following list, consider not only the roles that directly support the challenges and opportunities before you, but also the role of custodial leader and the enabling roles of trusting leader, trusted leader, and nurturing leader. Again we emphasize the importance of focusing on and further developing these roles as they help establish the trust, confidence, and comfort that serve as the foundation for your leadership:

- Custodial leader
- Trusted leader
- Trusting leader
- Nurturing leader
- Strategic leader
- Supportive leader
- Developmental leader
- Inspiring leader
- Working leader

Once you have identified the select few areas on which to focus your attention and direct your effort, you must take immediate action, or a change in your behavior—either as a practicing leader or in your attempt to further develop your leadership abilities—is not likely to occur. We recommend that you set the stage for change by completing the following tables. They list opportunities (for example, meetings and one-on-one interactions) for you to emphasize leadership actions. Place a check mark by each action you feel will contribute to your successfully leading your organization within its current context. This is not an all-inclusive list; while completing this table be sure to insert into the blank spaces other opportunities to emphasize leadership actions that you feel exist within your current situation. Consider your leadership as a light. Remember you can't shine it everywhere. Where do you *need* to shine it?

Table 11.1
Opportunities to Emphasize Custodial Leader Actions

	Meetings	One-on-One Interactions	Communications	Presentations
Custodial Leader				
Consider the long-term impact of your actions.	❑	❑	❑	❑
Focus on what has fueled past success.	❑	❑	❑	❑
Consider your impact on the environment.	❑	❑	❑	❑
Ensure that key challenges and triumphs are remembered.	❑	❑	❑	❑
Ensure that today's strengths are applied to future challenges and opportunities.	❑	❑	❑	❑
Identify the organization's heroes and ensure that their stories are known by all.	❑	❑	❑	❑
Record the "whys" of decisions so that they can be archived for future reference.	❑	❑	❑	❑
Protect what has transcended past generations and must transcend future generations.	❑	❑	❑	❑
Ensure creative and innovative ideas are celebrated, not simply tolerated.	❑	❑	❑	❑
Sometimes step aside as a leader, sometimes so as not to slow everyone else down.	❑	❑	❑	❑
Strive to sustain the organization for the long term.	❑	❑	❑	❑
Make certain the light of leadership in your organization never burns out.	❑	❑	❑	❑
Ensure a constant flow of leadership talent.	❑	❑	❑	❑
	❑	❑	❑	❑
	❑	❑	❑	❑
	❑	❑	❑	❑
	❑	❑	❑	❑

Table 11.2
Opportunities to Emphasize Trusted Leader Actions

Trusted Leader	Meetings	One-on-One Interactions	Communications	Presentations
Tell the truth, the whole truth, and nothing but the truth.	❏	❏	❏	❏
Lead by example.	❏	❏	❏	❏
Admit your mistakes.	❏	❏	❏	❏
Collaborate with others.	❏	❏	❏	❏
Keep your promises.	❏	❏	❏	❏
Do not expend needless energy blaming others.	❏	❏	❏	❏
Spend time building people up instead of tearing them down.	❏	❏	❏	❏
Do not motivate by fear.	❏	❏	❏	❏
Consider the needs of others first.	❏	❏	❏	❏
Consistently be open and honest, even when it "hurts."	❏	❏	❏	❏
Ask those closest to you to take the same risks you are asking of others.	❏	❏	❏	❏
Advocate for your people.	❏	❏	❏	❏
Share your fears.	❏	❏	❏	❏
Assess your intentions.	❏	❏	❏	❏
Accurately communicate the opinions of others even when you disagree.	❏	❏	❏	❏
Be consistent in your actions.	❏	❏	❏	❏
	❏	❏	❏	❏
	❏	❏	❏	❏
	❏	❏	❏	❏

Table 11.3
Opportunities to Emphasize Trusting Leader Actions

	Meetings	One-on-One Interactions	Communications	Presentations
Trusting Leader				
Allow others to lead.	❏	❏	❏	❏
Give others permission to make mistakes.	❏	❏	❏	❏
Reinforce good performance.	❏	❏	❏	❏
Celebrate the achievement of others.	❏	❏	❏	❏
Allow others to fail even when the risk is great.	❏	❏	❏	❏
Give authority to people to whom you have given responsibility.	❏	❏	❏	❏
Do not punish the bearer of bad news.	❏	❏	❏	❏
Act on others' ideas when appropriate.	❏	❏	❏	❏
Seek ideas from others.	❏	❏	❏	❏
Focus on the goal and let others worry about the how.	❏	❏	❏	❏
Trust what others are saying to you, even when you have doubts.	❏	❏	❏	❏
When appropriate, act on the advice of others, even when you strongly disagree with them.	❏	❏	❏	❏
Recognize that people's fears are their realities.	❏	❏	❏	❏
Trust others enough to share your leadership responsibilities.	❏	❏	❏	❏
	❏	❏	❏	❏
	❏	❏	❏	❏
	❏	❏	❏	❏

Table 11.4
Opportunities to Emphasize Nurturing Leader Actions

	Meetings	One-on-One Interactions	Communications	Presentations
Nurturing Leader				
Work to establish a sense of "family" within your organization.	❑	❑	❑	❑
Regularly check how everyone is doing emotionally, psychologically, and physically.	❑	❑	❑	❑
Learn from your direct reports, encouraging them to share their skills.	❑	❑	❑	❑
Encourage people around you to more broadly share their skills.	❑	❑	❑	❑
Focus your attention on the immediate needs of the people.	❑	❑	❑	❑
Focus your attention on calming the fears of people.	❑	❑	❑	❑
Strive to understand and reduce the limitations of others.	❑	❑	❑	❑
Spend time helping people get "little doses" of the challenges facing them.	❑	❑	❑	❑
Reassure others that regardless of what happens, "we remain a united family."	❑	❑	❑	❑
Ensure the voice of the minority is heard and taken into consideration.	❑	❑	❑	❑
Understand the limitations you and your people have.	❑	❑	❑	❑
Focus more on people's development.	❑	❑	❑	❑
Take steps to ensure that people are proud of how they are developing.	❑	❑	❑	❑
Show individuals the progress they are making.	❑	❑	❑	❑
Be honest about people's abilities when you focus on developing people.	❑	❑	❑	❑
	❑	❑	❑	❑
	❑	❑	❑	❑
	❑	❑	❑	❑

Table 11.5
Opportunities to Emphasize Strategic Leader Actions

Strategic Leader	Meetings	One-on-One Interactions	Communications	Presentations
Keep an eye on the competition.	❏	❏	❏	❏
Learn more about your industry.	❏	❏	❏	❏
Reinvent your industry instead of trying simply to lead it.	❏	❏	❏	❏
Accept input from other sources.	❏	❏	❏	❏
Try to see things from a different perspective.	❏	❏	❏	❏
Share what you see with others.	❏	❏	❏	❏
Involve more people in defining the vision/strategy.	❏	❏	❏	❏
Decide where you are headed.	❏	❏	❏	❏
Focus everyone's attention on where you are going.	❏	❏	❏	❏
Show people the boundaries within which they operate.	❏	❏	❏	❏
Stress the urgent need for people to move forward.	❏	❏	❏	❏
Highlight the advantages to moving forward.	❏	❏	❏	❏
Clearly describe the hazards of the path forward.	❏	❏	❏	❏
Help others focus on the overall mission rather than on the day-to-day challenges and crises.	❏	❏	❏	❏
	❏	❏	❏	❏
	❏	❏	❏	❏
	❏	❏	❏	❏

Table 11.6
Opportunities to Emphasize Supportive Leader Actions

	Meetings	One-on-One Interactions	Communications	Presentations
Supportive Leader				
Provide people with a comprehensive view of the destination and the obstacles and challenges.	❑	❑	❑	❑
Consistently communicate key messages to all areas and levels of the organization.	❑	❑	❑	❑
Set a pace to allow everyone to "keep up."	❑	❑	❑	❑
Give people sufficient time to try their ideas.	❑	❑	❑	❑
Make certain you have sufficiently budgeted to allow new ideas to be fully and thoroughly implemented.	❑	❑	❑	❑
Make certain that people are linked together in their efforts.	❑	❑	❑	❑
Make certain the workload is balanced for everyone.	❑	❑	❑	❑
Reorganize your teams for more effective performance.	❑	❑	❑	❑
Make certain that people who need extra support get it.	❑	❑	❑	❑
Make certain that you adequately supply people with the tools they need.	❑	❑	❑	❑
Reassure people that they will have access to what they need to succeed.	❑	❑	❑	❑
Personally sacrifice for the "common" good in times of extreme crisis.	❑	❑	❑	❑
Clarify the process for moving forward and ensuring everyone's success.	❑	❑	❑	❑
Empower people to take action.	❑	❑	❑	❑
	❑	❑	❑	❑
	❑	❑	❑	❑
	❑	❑	❑	❑

Table 11.7
Opportunities to Emphasize Developmental Leader Actions

	Meetings	One-on-One Interactions	Communications	Presentations
Developmental Leader				
Give people the chance to learn from others' expertise.	❏	❏	❏	❏
In addition to celebrating successes, share "lessons" with others so that, they, too may learn from your experiences.	❏	❏	❏	❏
Find out what people have to contribute.	❏	❏	❏	❏
Give people a chance to discover how to accomplish their objectives.	❏	❏	❏	❏
Solicit input from others.	❏	❏	❏	❏
Give others the opportunity to plot the path forward.	❏	❏	❏	❏
Allow people to contribute the expertise they have collected from other experiences.	❏	❏	❏	❏
Give people an opportunity for broader experiences.	❏	❏	❏	❏
Ask others their perception of what your role should be.	❏	❏	❏	❏
Give people the chance to examine their challenges from a different perspective.	❏	❏	❏	❏
Challenge the group so they think in more creative and innovative ways.	❏	❏	❏	❏
Understand the capabilities of your group.	❏	❏	❏	❏
	❏	❏	❏	❏
	❏	❏	❏	❏
	❏	❏	❏	❏
	❏	❏	❏	❏

Table 11.8
Opportunities to Emphasize Inspiring Leader Actions

Inspiring Leader	Meetings	One-on-One Interactions	Communications	Presentations
Show people how close they are to reaching their destination.	❏	❏	❏	❏
Remind people their destination is better than where they currently are.	❏	❏	❏	❏
Reinforce that people are not alone in the challenges they face and that everyone will share together in the eventual rewards.	❏	❏	❏	❏
Remind people of the dream that started them out on this journey.	❏	❏	❏	❏
Remind people that, by working together, any obstacles will be easily overcome.	❏	❏	❏	❏
Remind people of what they have accomplished so far.	❏	❏	❏	❏
Remind people they have already overcome much more challenging situations.	❏	❏	❏	❏
Exhibit the confidence and drive needed to inspire others.	❏	❏	❏	❏
Find out what your people do best and link it to the dream.	❏	❏	❏	❏
Give people the opportunity to do what they do best, in pursuit of the dream.	❏	❏	❏	❏
Articulate your dream, along with the dreams of the organization.	❏	❏	❏	❏
Spend time encouraging others.	❏	❏	❏	❏
	❏	❏	❏	❏
	❏	❏	❏	❏
	❏	❏	❏	❏

Table 11.9
Opportunities to Emphasize Working Leader Actions

	Meetings	One-on-One Interactions	Communications	Presentations
Working Leader				
Help align everyone to the common goal.	❑	❑	❑	❑
Focus on the details.	❑	❑	❑	❑
Monitor, measure, and communicate progress.	❑	❑	❑	❑
Balance "hard" and "soft" measures.	❑	❑	❑	❑
Be measurement driven.	❑	❑	❑	❑
Work among—and with—others to solve problems.	❑	❑	❑	❑
Help people differentiate between crises and mere inconveniences.	❑	❑	❑	❑
Find out what others are having difficulty with and what they are finding easy.	❑	❑	❑	❑
As needed, spend time down in the details.	❑	❑	❑	❑
Manufacture quick victories.	❑	❑	❑	❑
Make certain you adequately supply people with the tools they need.	❑	❑	❑	❑
Remain mentally agile and apply personal creativity to the situation at hand.	❑	❑	❑	❑
Devote time to accurately assess the contributions you make as "Leader."	❑	❑	❑	❑
Let people know you are open to suggestions and recommendations.	❑	❑	❑	❑
At the end of the day, review today's actions and plan for tomorrow.	❑	❑	❑	❑
	❑	❑	❑	❑
	❑	❑	❑	❑
	❑	❑	❑	❑

DIAGNOSING COMPETENCIES TO LEVERAGE AND DEVELOP

These tables list competencies you should emphasize when initially functioning within a particular context and those competencies you should emphasize once progress is made. The competencies are organized by role, with some competencies generally applicable across all roles. Use the results of the previous activities to identify the context in which you are leading and then identify leadership roles most likely to benefit your leadership efforts. Once you have done that, determine the competencies you will target for further development. When selecting and marking competencies, we recommend that you choose one or two strengths you can further leverage and one or two competencies you should further develop. Consider this a way of improving the *intensity* of your leadership light.

Table 11.10
Start Up a New Organization

Initially emphasize...	*As progress is made emphasize...*
General	General
❑ Interpersonal Communication	❑ Organizational Savvy
❑ Managing Others	
❑ Organizational Savvy	
Nurturing	Nurturing
❑ Relationship Management	❑ Relationship Management
❑ Respecting Diversity	❑ Respecting Diversity
Trusted	
❑ Courage of Convictions	
❑ Integrity	
Strategic	
❑ Business Acumen	
❑ Customer Focus	
❑ Visioning	
Working	
❑ Driving for Results	
❑ In-Depth Problem Solving	
	Custodial
	❑ Resilience
	❑ Courage of Convictions
	Trusting
	❑ Relationship Management
	❑ Respecting Diversity
	Supportive
	❑ Managing Others
	❑ Planning & Organizing
	Developmental
	❑ Continuous Learning
	❑ Coaching & Developing Others

Table 11.11
Take an Organization in a New Direction from a Successful State When People Are Open to Change

Initially emphasize...	*As progress is made emphasize...*
General	General
❏ Interpersonal Communication	❏ Interpersonal Communication
❏ Championing Change	❏ Championing Change
Custodial	Custodial
❏ Resilience	❏ Resilience
❏ Courage of Convictions	❏ Courage of Convictions
Trusting	Trusting
❏ Relationship Management	❏ Relationship Management
❏ Respecting Diversity	❏ Respecting Diversity
Strategic	
❏ Business Acumen	
❏ Customer Focus	
❏ Visioning	
Supportive	
❏ Managing Others	
❏ Planning & Organizing	
	Developmental
	❏ Continuous Learning
	❏ Coaching & Developing Others
	Nurturing
	❏ Relationship Management
	❏ Respecting Diversity
	Inspiring
	❏ Influencing & Persuading
	❏ Motivating Others

Table 11.12
Take an Organization in a New Direction from a Successful State When People Are Resistant to Change

Initially emphasize...	*As progress is made emphasize...*
General	General
❑ Interpersonal Communication	❑ Interpersonal Communication
❑ Championing Change	❑ Championing Change
Trusted	Trusted
❑ Courage of Convictions	❑ Courage of Convictions
❑ Integrity	❑ Integrity
Strategic	Strategic
❑ Business Acumen	❑ Business Acumen
❑ Customer Focus	❑ Customer Focus
❑ Visioning	❑ Visioning
Supportive	Supportive
❑ Managing Others	❑ Managing Others
❑ Planning & Organizing	❑ Planning & Organizing
Working	
❑ Driving for Results	
❑ In-Depth Problem Solving	
	Custodial
	❑ Resilience
	❑ Courage of Convictions

Table 11.13
Take an Organization in a New Direction from a Failed State

Initially emphasize…	*As progress is made emphasize…*
General	General
❏ Interpersonal Communication	❏ Interpersonal Communication
❏ Championing Change	❏ Championing Change
Trusted	Trusted
❏ Courage of Convictions	❏ Courage of Convictions
❏ Integrity	❏ Integrity
Strategic	
❏ Business Acumen	
❏ Customer Focus	
❏ Visioning	
Supportive	
❏ Managing Others	
❏ Planning & Organizing	
Working	
❏ Driving for Results	
❏ In-Depth Problem Solving	
	Nurturing
	❏ Relationship Management
	❏ Respecting Diversity
	Trusting
	❏ Relationship Management
	❏ Respecting Diversity
	Developmental
	❏ Continuous Learning
	❏ Coaching & Developing Others
	Inspiring
	❏ Influencing & Persuading
	❏ Motivating Others

Table 11.14
Maintain a Current Path/State

Initially emphasize...

General
- [ ] Interpersonal Communication
- [ ] Teamwork & Collaboration

Custodial
- [ ] Resilience
- [ ] Courage of Convictions
- [ ] Organizational Savvy

Trusting
- [ ] Relationship Management
- [ ] Respecting Diversity

Nurturing
- [ ] Relationship Management
- [ ] Respecting Diversity

Developmental
- [ ] Continuous Learning
- [ ] Coaching & Developing Others

Supportive
- [ ] Managing Others
- [ ] Planning & Organizing

Table 11.15
New Person Required to Maintain a Current Path/State

Initially emphasize...

General
- ❏ Interpersonal Communication
- ❏ Teamwork & Collaboration

Custodial
- ❏ Resilience
- ❏ Organizational Savvy

Trusted
- ❏ Integrity

Trusting
- ❏ Relationship Management
- ❏ Respecting Diversity

Developmental
- ❏ Continuous Learning
- ❏ Coaching & Developing Others

Supportive
- ❏ Managing Others
- ❏ Planning & Organizing

CONCLUSION

This chapter has allowed you to give some careful thought to what you are hoping to accomplish and the context within which you function. This analysis undoubtedly has helped you:

- Crystallize your understanding of the assumptions and expectations your particular circumstances bring with them
- Identify leadership roles you will need to emphasize when attempting to address those particular assumptions and expectations

It has also helped you identify:

- The three or four leadership roles you should emphasize to maximize your leadership performance and to optimize the extent to which you will be able to influence your followers. This will help you decide where to shine your leadership light.
- The three or four leadership competencies you must target if you wish to develop your leadership abilities in an effective and efficient manner, given the context within which you operate. This will help you improve the intensity of the leadership light you shine.

You now have concrete information on which to base leadership actions and leadership development activities. You will incorporate this information into your development plan (described in Chapter 12) and action plan (described in Chapter 13). Resources you should consider taking advantage of as you pursue your leadership objectives and strive to further develop your leadership skills are included in Chapter 14.

TWELVE

Development Plan

This book is based on the belief that tackling today's myriad of challenges requires a certain mindset, awareness, and nimbleness on behalf of the person thinking and acting as a leader. Whether you are a professional or nonprofessional, supervisor, manager, or executive, to successfully address these challenges your thoughts, words, and actions must be both planned and purposeful. We will say it again: we believe the most challenging aspect of leadership does not relate to the technical knowledge of your business or functional area; rather, it relates to the roles you must play as a leader and the leadership actions you must take to succeed in the variety of contexts within which you will function throughout your career.

Chapters 11, 12, and 13 require an investment of your time. Assuming your workday is already hectic, we encourage you to diagnose your present conditions and circumstance, create your personal development plan, and develop your action plan only if you are likely to put them to use. If you must occasionally influence those around you in a way that causes them to perform at a level they otherwise would not have deemed possible, proceed forward. If you are serious about further developing your ability to influence others in such a manner, proceed forward.

We feel that a quick recap of what we have already covered in this book is now in order. The first nine chapters introduced:

- Nine leadership roles and related actions and behaviors
- Six organizational contexts and the unique demands and expectations each exert on the leader
- 23 competencies that relate to the leadership roles

We consider this information to be the underpinning of leadership performance. Building on these earlier chapters, Chapter 11 introduced a process you can use to diagnose your organizational context and determine the leadership roles and competencies most appropriate for your prevailing context. Chapters 12 and 13 are about action. They introduce information, processes, and tools you can use to select leadership actions and competencies to emphasize and further develop, given your current context. With a focus on utility and applicability, this chapter presents information and a tool you can use to enhance your leadership ability. Chapter 13 presents an action plan you can use when attempting to integrate your development plan into your daily work life.

The next two chapters will help you achieve the change you desire to have greater influence on your followers and your organization. Such change and desired results will not simply occur. Change requires effort that you must put forth within the context of your busy and hectic workday. You must therefore do all that you can to help yourself take the time you need to put your newly gained knowledge into action. You must help yourself recognize opportunities that surface on a daily basis likely to allow you to apply that action to organizational situations and circumstances. Such change does not occur in a vacuum; it will occur within the:

- Constraints, obstacles, and challenges that confront you on a daily basis
- Advantageous circumstances and situations that avail themselves to you each day

The results you desire will also occur within the complexity of your typical work day: they will result *in spite of* the acute constraints, obstacles, and challenges and *because of* the advantageous situations. The personal development plan will sensitize you to what you must do to become a more effective leader and will alert you to (1) those advantageous situations you must capitalize on and (2) those constraints, obstacles, and challenges you must acknowledge and work to turn into opportunities.

PLANNING FOR PERSONAL DEVELOPMENT

Many readers may feel that the need for creating a personal development plan does not exist—that intent and effort will suffice. To those readers, we ask you to consider past failed attempts to change your behavior; perhaps changes in behavior decided on during your most recent New Years Eve. Although you may decide a particular change is important or that a particular change may be beneficial, intent alone is seldom enough. Think of your most significant accomplishments. Odds are they did not occur through happenstance but were the result of a well-thought-out and well-executed plan.

The personal development plan is designed to help you focus on the intended changes in your behavior and to allow you, in a planned and purposeful way, to bring support resources to bear on the behavior or action you wish to change. Focusing in such a way and taking advantage of your support system will allow you to translate your intent of becoming a more effective leader into action.

The leadership model we have introduced in this book is based on the need to match leadership roles with organizational contexts. This suggests the need for leadership behaviors and actions to "fit" the unique set of circumstances (along with the associated demands, needs, and expectations) inherent to a specific situation. The same is true of the personal development plan: the actions it recommends cannot be generic in nature or they will not be specific enough to apply or to be of any use. Nor can they apply to all situations.

The personal development plan must reflect the results of your diagnosis and analysis. The actions listed in the personal development plan must make sense to you, given what you are asked to do on a daily basis and in accordance to the unique demands, needs, and expectations relating to your particular context. The personal development plan must focus on the leader you hope (no, that you plan) to become. It must focus on current circumstances, because they represent the context within which you must function and the context within which your leadership growth and development will occur. The personal development plan must be detailed and specific enough for *you* to put into action. Such action typically requires you to plan in advance, prepare to capitalize on advantageous situations, and stand ready to apply newly acquired leadership skills to constraints, challenges, and obstacles.

THE PERSONAL DEVELOPMENT PLAN

Information provided in Chapter 11 allows you to give some careful thought to what you are hoping to accomplish and the context within which you function. This analysis undoubtedly helped you:

- Crystallize your understanding of the assumptions and expectations your particular circumstances bring with them

- Identify leadership roles you will need to emphasize when attempting to address those particular assumptions and expectations

It has also helped you identify:

- The three or four leadership roles that you should emphasize to maximize your leadership performance and to optimize the extent to which you will be able to influence your followers
- The three or four leadership competencies that you must target if you wish to develop your leadership abilities in an effective and efficient manner, given the context within which you operate

The personal development plan shown here will help you focus your attention and put forth the effort needed to emphasize leadership roles most appropriate for your current context. Feel free to modify this personal development plan or replace it with one that you have previously used. Either way, be sure to link it back to the results of your diagnosis from Chapter 11 and include concrete actions. Actions are sufficiently concrete if you can share them with someone else and that person can describe to you what you intend to do or how your behavior will appear to others.

As previously stressed, changes in your leadership behavior and your being able to influence others in a more effective manner will not simply occur. Your completing and utilizing this personal development plan requires effort that you must put forth within the context of your busy and hectic work day. This personal development plan will help you capitalize on advantageous situations that avail themselves to you each day and keep you from falling victim to the constraints, obstacles, and challenges that will undoubtedly confront you. We encourage you to complete and use a personal development plan. It will help you take the time you need to put your newly gained knowledge into action, and help you recognize those countless opportunities that surface on a daily basis likely to allow you to apply that action to organizational situations.

Table 12.1
Personal Development Plan

From the diagnosis you completed in Chapter 11, insert below the three or four leadership roles you wish to further develop. For each role, list related competencies, behaviors and actions.

	Leadership Roles Targeted for Immediate Application or for Further Development	*Related Competencies, Behaviors, Actions*
1		
2		
3		
4		

For Leadership Role #1, write a developmental goal that is both specific and measurable.

_____
_____
_____

Describe how you will achieve this developmental goal. Include actions that are specific and observable.

_____
_____
_____

Describe the situations and circumstances that will allow you to display these actions. To the extent possible predict when those opportunities are likely to appear.

_____
_____
_____

List two or three individuals who may be in a position to offer assistance or provide feedback, in terms of your displaying the actions (described above) in these particular situations and under these particular circumstances.

_____

_____

_____

Describe what assistance or feedback you will solicit from these individuals.

_____

_____

_____

Set a target completion date: _____ Keep this date in mind; it will help sensitize you to the need to think about the goal, the importance of taking action, and the necessity of soliciting the assistance of others.

For Leadership Role #2, write a developmental goal that is both specific and measurable.

_____

_____

_____

Describe how you will achieve this developmental goal. Include actions that are specific and observable.

_____

_____

_____

Describe the situations and circumstances that will allow you to display these actions. To the extent possible predict when those opportunities are likely to appear.

_____

_____

_____

List two or three individuals who may be in a position to offer assistance or provide feedback, in terms of your displaying the actions (described above) in these particular situations and under these particular circumstances.

_____

_____

_____

Describe what assistance or feedback you will solicit from these individuals.

_____

_____

_____

Set a target completion date: _____ Keep this date in mind; it will help sensitize you to the need to think about the goal, the importance of taking action, and the necessity of soliciting the assistance of others.

For Leadership Role #3, write a developmental goal that is both specific and measurable.

_____

_____

_____

Describe how you will achieve this developmental goal. Include actions that are specific and observable.

_____

_____

_____

Describe the situations and circumstances that will allow you to display these actions. To the extent possible predict when those opportunities are likely to appear.

_____

_____

_____

List two or three individuals who may be in a position to offer assistance or provide feedback, in terms of your displaying the actions (described above) in these particular situations and under these particular circumstances.

_____

_____

_____

Describe what assistance or feedback you will solicit from these individuals.

_____

_____

_____

Set a target completion date: _____ Keep this date in mind; it will help sensitize you to the need to think about the goal, the importance of taking action, and the necessity of soliciting the assistance of others.

For Leadership Role #4, write a developmental goal that is both specific and measurable.

_____

_____

_____

Describe how you will achieve this developmental goal. Include actions that are specific and observable.

_____

_____

_____

Describe the situations and circumstances that will allow you to display these actions. To the extent possible predict when those opportunities are likely to appear.

_____

_____

_____

List two or three individuals who may be in a position to offer assistance or provide feedback, in terms of your displaying the actions (described above) in these particular situations and under these particular circumstances.

_____

_____

_____

Describe what assistance or feedback you will solicit from these individuals.

_____

_____

_____

Set a target completion date: _____ Keep this date in mind; it will help sensitize you to the need to think about the goal, the importance of taking action, and the necessity of soliciting the assistance of others.

THIRTEEN

Action Plan

Like Chapter 12, this chapter is about action. You now have a personal development plan that will be useful only if you apply it to your everyday work life. In addition, implementing your personal development plan is not an end unto itself; its purpose is to support you as you work to change your leadership behavior in a manner that will give you greater influence on your followers and your organization. In other words, we encourage you to further develop your leadership capabilities and use your strengthened leadership capabilities to continue to improve your organization.

You must therefore do all that you can to recognize daily opportunities that allow you to apply contextual leadership actions in your organizational setting. Be aware of the organizational terrain around you and be nimble enough to capitalize on advantageous circumstances that avail themselves to you. Do not fall victim to the constraints, obstacles, and challenges that confront you on a daily basis; take advantage of them!

The action plan outlined here will help you focus your attention and put forth the effort needed to emphasize leadership roles most appropriate for your current context. It builds on information resulting from your diagnosis in Chapter 11 and your development plan in Chapter 12. It allows you to plan for opportunities to work on, hone, and apply new and improved leadership skills.

Space is provided in the plan for you to insert up to five additional situations likely to avail themselves to you, given your current context. Insert information into that space; it will allow you to further identify scenarios likely to surface in advance, plan for their occurrence, and prepare to apply the leadership actions appropriate for those particular situations. Feel free to modify this action plan or replace it with one that you have previously used.

As you firm up your diagnosis, personal development plan, and action plan, you might be interested in obtaining additional information on leadership. Chapter 14 presents a number of leadership resources you may find interesting, useful, and beneficial.

Table 13.1
Action Plan

Review your personal development plan and the results of your diagnosis.
From your personal development plan, note the three or four leadership roles you should emphasize, given your organizational context.

_____

_____

_____

_____

From the diagnosis, review the list of opportunities (Meetings, One-on-One Interactions, Communications, and Presentations) for displaying those particular roles. Take this into consideration as you complete the following sections.

For each of the following situations, describe how you plan to apply contextual leadership actions to enhance your ability to influence your followers.

Meetings

Action	How	When

One-on-one Interactions

Action	How	When

Communications

Action	How	When

Presentations

Action	How	When

Action	How	When

Action	How	When

Action	How	When

Action	How	When

FOURTEEN

Resources for the Manager as Leader

The previous chapters contributed to your creating a personal development plan and an action plan. Combined, they help you capitalize on opportunities to apply newly acquired leadership skills and abilities. As you test and practice those new skills and abilities, you may wish to continue exploring the subject of leadership. If this is the case, the following resources may prove useful and beneficial to you.

BOOKS

Ackerman, Laurence D. *Identity is Destiny: Leadership and the Roots of Value Creation.* San Francisco, Calif.: Berrett-Koehler Publishers, 2000.

Bennis, Warren. *On Becoming a Leader.* New York: Addison Wesley, 1989.

Covey, Stephen R. *Principle-Centered Leadership.* New York: Simon & Schuster, 1992.

Dotlich, David L., and Peter C. Cario. *Unnatural Leadership: Going Against Intuition and Experience to Develop Ten New Leadership Instincts.* San Francisco, Calif.: Jossey-Bass, 2002.

Farkas, Charles M., and Philippe De Backer. *Maximum Leadership: The World's Leading CEOs Share Their Five Strategies for Success.* New York: Henry Holt & Company, 1996.

Hersey, Paul, and Ken Blanchard. *Management of Organizational Behavior,* 4th ed. Englewood Cliffs, N.J.: Prentice-Hall, 1982.

Hughes, Richard L., Robert C. Ginnett, and Gordon J. Curphy. *Leadership: Enhancing the Lessons of Experience.* New York: Irwin McGraw-Hill, 1999.

Krzyzewski, Mike. *Leading with the Heart.* New York: Warner Books, 2000.

Marquardt, Michael J., and Nancy O. Berger. *Global Leaders for the 21st Century.* New York: SUNY Press, 2000.

Rhinesmith, Stephen H. *A Manager's Guide to Globilization: Six Skills for Success in a Changing World,* 2nd ed. New York: McGraw-Hill, 1996.

Rosenbach, William E., and Robert L. Taylor. *Contemporary Issues in Leadership,* 5th ed. Boulder, Colo.: Westview Press, 2001.

Sayles, Leonard R. *Leadership: Managing in Real Organizations,* 2nd ed. New York: McGraw-Hill, 1989.

Tichy, Noel M. *The Leadership Engine: How Winning Companies Build Leaders at Every Level.* New York: HarperCollins, 1997.

Watkins, Michael. *The First 90 Days: Critical Success Strategies for New Leaders at All Levels.* Boston: Harvard Business School Press, 2003.

Yukl, Gary A. *Leadership in Organizations.* Englewood Cliffs, N.J.: Prentice-Hall, 1981.

JOURNALS AND MAGAZINES

The Academy of Management Executive
Organization: The Academy of Management
Frequency: Published quarterly
ISSN: 0896–3789
Subscribe: Telephone (800) 633 4931 or
   email aom@exchange.ebsco.com

The Academy of Management Journal
Organization: The Academy of Management
Frequency: Published six times a year
ISSN: 0001–4273
Subscribe: Telephone (800) 633 4931 or
   email aom@exchange.ebsco.com

The Academy of Management Review
Organization: The Academy of Management
Frequency: Published quarterly
ISSN: 0363–7425
Subscribe: Telephone (800) 633 4931 or
    email aom@exchange.ebsco.com

Harvard Business Review
Organization: Harvard Business School
Frequency: Published monthly, except for a July/August issue that
    counts as two issues
ISSN: 0017–8012
Subscribe: Telephone (800) 274 3214 or email hbursubs@neodata.com

Leader to Leader
Organization: Leader to Leader Institute
Frequency: Published quarterly
ISSN: 1087–8149
Subscribe: Telephone (888) 378 2537 or email jbsubs@jbp.com

Leadership Excellence
Organization: Executive Excellence Publishing
Frequency: Published monthly
ISSN: 8756–2308
Subscribe: Telephone (800) 304 9782 or email info@eep.com

Management Science
Organization: Institute for Operations Research and the Management
    Sciences
Frequency: Published monthly.
ISSN: 0025–1909
Subscribe: Email informs@informs.org

Sloan Management Review
Organization: MIT Sloan School of Management
Frequency: Published quarterly
ISSN: 0019–848X
Subscribe: Telephone (800) 875 5764 or email SLON@neodata.com

Strategy & Business
Organization: Booz, Allen, & Hamilton, Inc.
Frequency: Published quarterly
ISSN: 1083–706X
Subscribe: Telephone (877) 829 9108 or
    email strategy_business@neodata.com

ORGANIZATIONS

Academy of Management
P.O. Box 3020
Briarcliff Manor, NY 10510–8020 (USA)
Phone: (914) 923 2607
Fax: (914) 923 2615
Email: aom@pace.edu
Website: http://www.aomonline.org

Center for Creative Leadership
One Leadership Place
Post Office Box 26300
Greensboro, NC, USA 27438–6300
Phone: (336) 545 2810
Fax: (336) 282 3284
Email: info@leaders.ccl.org
Website: http://www.ccl.org

Institute for Operations Research and the
    Management Sciences (INFORMS)
7240 Parkway Drive, Suite 310
Hanover, MD, USA 21076
Phone: (443) 757 3500
Fax: (443) 757 3515
Email: informs@informs.org
Website: http://www.informs.org/

Strategic Management Society
Purdue University—Krannert Center
425 W. State Street

West Lafayette, IN, USA 47907
Phone: (765) 494 6984
Fax: (765) 494 1533
Email: sms@exchange.purdue.edu
Website: http://www.smsweb.org/

Young Presidents' Organization
Global Services Center
Hickok Center
451 S. Decker Drive
Irving, TX 75062
Phone: (800) 773 7976
Email: askypo@ypo.org
Website: http://www.ypo.org

ARTICLES

Bennis, Warren. "The Leadership Advantage." *Leader to Leader* 12 (Spring 1999): 18–23.
Graeff, C. L. "Evolution of Situational Leadership Theory: A Critical Review." *Leadership Quarterly* 8 (1997): 153–70.
Hersey P., and K. Blanchard. "So You Want to Know Your Leadership Style?" *Training and Development Journal* February (1974): 1–15.
House, R. J. "A Path-Goal Theory of Leader Effectiveness." *Administrative Science Quarterly* September (1971): 321–38.

ARTICLES AVAILABLE ONLINE

Bartlett, Christopher A. and Meg Wozney. "GE's Two-Decade Transformation: Jack Welch's Leadership," *Harvard Business Review,* Published April 28, 1999. Product number 9–399–150 available from Harvard Business Online (http://harvardbusinessonline).
Bennis, Warren G. "The Crucibles of Leadership." *Harvard Business Review,* Published September 1, 2002. Product number R0209B available from Harvard Business Online (http://harvardbusinessonline).
Bennis, Warren G. "The Seven Ages of the Leader." *Harvard Business Review,* Published January 1, 2004. Product number R0401D available from Harvard Business Online (http://harvardbusinessonline).

Kanter, Rosabeth Moss. "Leadership for Change: Enduring Skills for Change Masters." *Harvard Business Review,* Published November 25, 2003. Product number 9–304–062 available from Harvard Business Online (http://harvardbusinessonline).

Kaplan, Robert S., and David P. Norton, "Organizational Capital: Leadership, Alignment, and Teamwork." *Harvard Business Review,* Published March 15, 2004. Product number B0403A available from Harvard Business Online (http://harvardbusinessonline).

Mintzberg, Henry. "Enough Leadership." *Harvard Business Review,* Published November 1, 2004. Product number F0411D available from Harvard Business Online (http://harvardbusinessonline).

ADDITIONAL RESOURCES

A recent Internet search of the term *leadership* produced 520,000,000 results, and the term *leader* produced 344,000,000. If you wish to explore further, take a few minutes to research "leadership" and "leader" using your favorite Internet search engine, college learning resource center, or local public library. The results you attain will provide a plethora of additional references and resources. These will undoubtedly appeal to those of you interested in learning more about leadership and about what you might do to more effectively influence your followers to accomplish what they otherwise would not have deemed possible.

Notes

Chapter 1

1. Holly Dolezalek, "Industry Report 2004: Training Magazines 23rd Annual Comprehensive Analysis of Employer-Sponsored Training in the United States," *Training*, October 2004, 28.
2. Morgan W. McCall Jr., Michael M Lombard, and Ann M. Morrison, *The Lessons of Experience: How Successful Executives Develop on the Job* (New York: The Free Press, 1988).

Chapter 3

1. Coach K, "Coach K: The Official Website of Coach Mike Krzyzewski," http://www.coachk.com/
2. Nancy Humphrey, "Nurturing Leader: Deborah German Is Dedicated to Helping Vanderbilt Medical Students," *The Reporter*, August 31, 2002, http://www.mc.vanderbilt.edu/reporter/?id = 2224.
3. Linda A. Hill and Maria T. Farkas. *Meg Whitman and eBayGermany* (Harvard Business School Case Study 9–402–006) (Boston: Harvard Business School Publishing, 2001).
4. Autowitch, http://www.autowitch.org/?q = node/4025.

5. *Wikipedia Free Encyclopedia,* s.v. "Karl Wallenda," http://en.wikipedia.org/wiki/karl_wallenda (accessed October 29, 2005).
6. Estee Lauder Companies, Inc., "Heritage," http://www.elcompanies.com/heritage.asp.
7. Charles O'Reilly and Chrishan Thuraisingham, *Homestead Technologies: A Start-up Built to Last.* (Graduate School of Business, Stanford University Case Number HR-18) (Stanford, Calif.: Board of Trustees of the Leland Stanford Junior University, 2001).
8. Allen Narcisse, "Interview with Michael Lee-Chin," *The Harbus Online,* February 10, 2003, http://www.harbus.org/media/paper343/news/2003/02/10/news/interview.with.Michael.LeeChin-365187.shtml.

Chapter 4

1. Larry Weyers, interview by the author, September 30, 2005.

Chapter 5

1. Roy Morris, interview by the author, September 29, 2005.

Chapter 6

1. Derek Carissimi, interview by the author, September 19, 2005.

Chapter 7

1. Robert N. Munsch and Michael Martchenko (illustrator), *The Paper Bag Princess* (Toronto: Annick Press Ltd., 1980).

Chapter 8

1. Martha A. Stanford, interview by the author, September 22, 2005.

Chapter 10

1. Bigby, Havis & Associates, Inc. ASSESS&360° Competency Report. Dallas: Bigby, Havis & Associates, Inc., 2005.

Bibliography

Bennis, Warren and Burt Nanus. *Leaders: The Strategies for Taking Charge.* New York: Harper & Row, Publishers, 1985.

Bigby, Havis & Associates, Inc., *ASSESS&360° Competency Report,* Dallas: Bigby, Havis, and Associates, Inc, 2005.

Buckingham, Marcus and Curt Coffman. *First, Break all the Rules: What the World's Greatest Managers Do Differently.* New York: Simon & Schuster, 1999.

Coach K. "Coach K: The Official Website of Coach Mike Krzyzewski." http://www.coachk.com/.

Dolezalek, Holly. Industry Report 2004: Training Magazines 23rd Annual Comprehensive analysis of Employer-Sponsored Training in the United States. *Training,* October 2004, 28.

Estee Lauder Companies, Inc. *Heritage.* http://www.elcompanies.com/heritage.asp.

Hill, Linda A., and Maria T. Farkas. *Meg Whitman and eBayGermany.* (Harvard Business School Case Study 9–402–006). Boston: Harvard Business School Publishing, 2001.

Humphrey, Nancy. "Nurturing Leader: Deborah German Is Dedicated to Helping Vanderbilt Medical Students," *The Reporter,* August 31, 2002, http://www.mc.vanderbilt.edu/reporter/?id = 2224.

Kotter, John P. "What Leaders Really Do." *Harvard Business Review* 90, no. 3 (1990): 103–111.

———. *The Leadership Factor.* New York: The Free Press, 1988.

———. *Leading Change.* Boston: Harvard Business School Press, 1996.

Kouzes, James M., and Barry Z. Posner. *The Leadership Challenge: How to Keep Getting Extraordinary Things Done in Organizations.* San Francisco: Jossey-Bass Publishers, 1995.

Lucas, James R. *The Passionate Organization: Igniting the Fire of Employee Commitment.* New York: Amacom, 1999.

McCall, Morgan W., Jr., Michael M. Lombard, and Ann M. Morrison. *The Lessons of Experience: How Successful Executives Develop on the Job.* New York: The Free Press, 1988.

Munsch, Robert N., and Michael Martchenko (illustrator). *The Paper Bag Princess.* Toronto: Annick Press Ltd., 1980.

Narcisse, Allen. "Interview with Michael Lee-Chin," *The Harbus Online,* February 10, 2003, http://www.harbus.org/media/paper343/news/2003/02/10/news/interview.with.Michael.LeeChin-365187.shtml.

O'Reilly, Charles and Chrishan Thuraisingham. *Homestead Technologies: A Start-up Built to Last.* (Graduate School of Business, Stanford University Case Number HR-18). Stanford, CA: Board of Trustees of the Leland Stanford Junior University, 2001.

Index

About the Authors

B. KEITH SIMERSON, ED.D. A founding Partner of Tradewinds Consulting, LLC, B.K. has two decades of experience working for and consulting to Fortune 500 corporations and professional services firms. His areas of interest and expertise are change enablement, leadership development, strategic HR management, strategy formulation and execution, and organization development.

B.K. has served as an adjunct professor at Gardner-Webb University, guest lecturer at Webster University Graduate School, the Associate Editor of Police Chief (a professional journal with an international circulation of 40,000), has been a frequent presenter at conferences and seminars, has contributed materials to various journals (such as the Training Director's Forum), and was the lead author of Evaluating Police Management Development Programs (Praeger Publishers) and *Fired, Laid Off, Out of a Job: A Manual For Understanding, Coping, Surviving* (Greenwood Publishing Group).

B.K. earned his Ed.D., with an emphasis in management and organization development, from the University of North Carolina at Greensboro. He earned an M.A. with emphasis in administration, supervision, and higher education, from Appalachian State University. He also possesses B.A. and A.A.S. degrees and specialty certifications.

MICHAEL L. VENN, PH.D. A founding Partner of Tradewinds Consulting, LLC, Mike has more than 20 years of experience as a consultant, leader, and educator. He has worked for, and consulted to, numerous Fortune 500 and privately held companies. Mike's areas of interest and expertise are leadership development, strategy formulation and execution, change enablement, and organization development.

Mike has presented and taught globally on the topics ranging from leadership to the use of continuous improvement tools for planning and management. Mike contributed a chapter to *In Action: Conducting Needs Assessment* (American Society for Training and Development, Alexandria, Va.) and is the author of articles appearing in *Executive Excellence* and American Society of Training and Development and International Society for Performance and Improvement (ISPI) publications. Mike currently serves on the board of directors of the Association of Internal Management Consultants.

Mike earned his Ph.D., with an emphasis in computer-based training and testing, from the University of Illinois at Urbana-Champaign. He also earned an M.M. in Jazz Pedagogy from the University of Miami in Coral Gables, Florida and a B.S. in Music Education from the University of Illinois at Urbana-Champaign.

CPSIA information can be obtained at www.ICGtesting.com
Printed in the USA
BVOW010807270912

301384BV00006B/50/P